UNDER THE SIGN OF THE LILY

THE MESSIANIC SOPHIANIC AGE

Me · Me · Me
The Spider in the Web

The Law of Correspondence
and the Law of Projection

The Eternal Word,
the One God, the Free Spirit,
Speaks through Gabriele,
as through All the Prophets of God—
Abraham, Job, Moses, Elijah, Isaiah,
Jesus of Nazareth,
the Christ of God

Me • Me • Me
The Spider in the Web

*The Law of Correspondence
and the
Law of Projection*

Gabriele

Gabriele
Publishing House

Me. Me. Me.
The Spider in the Web
The Law of Correspondence
and the Law of Projection

2nd Edition, November 2021
© Gabriele-Verlag Das Wort GmbH
Max-Braun-Str. 02, 97828 Marktheidenfeld
www.gabriele-verlag.com
www.gabriele-publishing-house.com

Original German title:
"Ich, Ich, Ich, Die Spinne im Netz
Das Entsprechungsgesetz
und das Gesetz der Projection!"

The German edition is the work of reference for all
questions regarding the meaning of the contents

Translation authorized by
Gabriele-Verlag DAS WORT GmbH

Order No. S 325 en

Printed by: KlarDruck GmbH, Marktheidenfeld
ISBN 978-3-96446-230-5

Table of Contents

The ego of a person
can influence
his fellow human beings only until they
no longer pay tribute
to their own human ego
and raise their consciousness
more and more to God.
The baseness of a person
leaves him quickest
when he entrusts himself to God
in every situation.

Preface

There is great sadness in my heart for all my brothers and sisters who call themselves Christian, but do not honor the great Spirit, the Christ of God, by fulfilling His teaching, which He gave us as Jesus of Nazareth.

For more than 45 years, I have been privileged to experience how close God is to us. His almighty love, wisdom and greatness were personified in Jesus; and in the person Jesus, these were close to us people and we could hear and experience them in Him. With His life, He was the guarantor for the truth which He proclaimed and taught.

Jesus of Nazareth, a man from the tribe of David, brought us Redemption and the way into the Father's house. Jesus—a man's name, to identify the human being in the world, the "person." The person bore the impersonal, the nameless, the divine being, the Co-Regent of heaven, the part-power of the primordial power, omnipresent in the creative forces of the universe, the Son of God.

The eternal Spirit of love, wisdom and greatness took on a visible form in a Son of Man from the small town of Nazareth, the brother of his human brothers and sisters. His parents were Mary, a simple and modest woman, and Joseph, the carpenter. From him, the personified great Spirit of love and wisdom, the Christ of God in Jesus, learned the trade of a carpenter. If we would be aware of this context in its depth—Mary, the simple woman, Joseph, the carpenter from Nazareth, and his son, the carpenter, Jesus—then we could very gradually comprehend what God, our eternal Father, wanted to say to us through His Son, Jesus, the carpenter.

The great Spirit, the Christ of God, has been giving revelations through me for more than 45 years. I have an earthly name. But in my heart I am nameless, simply a sister among brothers and sisters. I am, I live and I serve in this awareness. Throughout the decades as the instrument of God, I have been privileged to experience over and over again what the Eternal wanted to say to us human beings through His Son, the carpenter, and what He wants to say anew today:

You do not need to study theology to experience God. God cannot be studied. Nor can He be found in theological studies, but solely in the nameless hearts of those who do not strive for rank, name, title and means, but simply open their heart for the great Spirit, which is the love, wisdom and greatness.

Christ, once the carpenter, Jesus, who led a simple life and was placed on an equal footing with His human brothers and sisters, who prayed and worked and who did not have a command of the spoken and written language of the "learned ones" of His time, cannot be found among those with a doctoral degree. He is not a link in the official chain, in which the "dignitaries" of this world have their place. Nor will we find Him on an artistically decorated cross set with gems, which the pope, the cardinals and bishops wear over their costly robes. He has neither the affected behavior of the families of emperors and kings nor is He in the upper ranks of the governments, not even when they kiss the pope's ring. He is not found at the intoxicating orgies of the rich, nor at the dissolute beer and wine drinking bouts of the middle class. He is also not the word of those who talk big about Christ and extol the Bible as the sole authority of the truth, but do not live according to it themselves.

The great Spirit, the Christ of God, is the nameless power of love, wisdom and greatness—nameless, even though we have given this power the name of Christ—which is consciously active in the hearts of those who bow before Him, the great Spirit, and fulfill His will more and more each day. They do not ask if they have to be worthy of this; they know that the one who thinks he is "worthy" of studying and representing His holy name is no Reverend Father, but presumptuous to the extreme. The "Reverend Father" wants to give the people an understanding of the great Spirit, once in the carpenter Jesus, but has not yet himself gotten his heart in proper shape so that the sole "worthy One" can be active in it.

The great nameless Spirit—we call it Christ— was in Jesus, the carpenter. He, the carpenter, had to bear the cross for all humankind. He had to, because the people, who did not care to fulfill the divine will, wanted it that way. It was not an elaborate cross decorated with precious stones, but a crude wooden cross, which expressed disgrace, because the one who was nailed to it was a criminal, a blot on society for the many onlookers who took pleasure in this excruciating event and considered it rightly done.

The person who becomes aware of the event of the crucifixion of Jesus of Nazareth gradually gains an inkling of what the Christ in Jesus did for all souls and people. Jesus had committed no sin, and He remained in the law, God, in the love, wisdom and greatness during His torture and crucifixion. Jesus allowed Himself to be killed. He did not rebel against it, although His Father, who is also our Father, could have sent legions of angels to spare His Son this disgrace and pain. God, the Eternal, did not do this. The incarnated high Spirit in Jesus was a man and thus, the Son of Man, which means: He was placed on an equal footing with all people.

Just as God did not intervene for His Son, although He was innocent when crucified, in the same way He does not intervene in our lives, in our sinfulness. Christ in Jesus brought us Redemption through His devotion to the eternal Father and to us human beings by personifying the great love of the eternal Father. In this, as it were, lies the statement: I love the Eternal with all My heart, with all My strength and with all My soul, and My brothers and sisters as Myself. I surrender, so that they may become lambs, who follow only the lamb of God, the great Shepherd, the Christ of God, who alone knows the way into the Father's house, and who, with His power, is the way, the truth and the life in their hearts.

As I write these accompanying words to this book, my heart becomes heavier and heavier, because I feel what our Redeemer, Christ, did for all souls and people and what He wanted. He, the Son of the Eternal, at the same time, brother to all people, sacrificed Himself, so that given His Redeemer-deed, we people would gain the strength—His nameless power of love, mercy and goodness—to find our way out of the prison of our ego, out of the network of our entanglements.

What have the Christians done during the past 2000 years? They have allowed themselves to be led astray by the leaders of the blind with the elaborate crosses on their breasts, away from the simple teaching of Jesus, the carpenter from Nazareth, to an artificial religion that is similar to the resplendent crosses, yet empty and cold.

My brothers and sisters all over the world, a nameless person, whom many simply address as Gabriele, calls to you to give honor to Christ, the great Spirit of love and wisdom, our Redeemer. Examnie it yourselves: Does theology with its dogmas bring you the water of life for which you thirst? Does it satisfy you with the bread of life, so that your days are peaceful and, in your deeds, fruitful? Does it give you the right direction and example for a meaningful life that is thankful from God and in God, and which merges into God after the physical death?

Brothers and sisters, I call to you, a sister, so to speak, who calls into the desert world: Open your hearts for Christ, who, as Jesus, was like you and me, plain and simple. He had a heart of gold. He loved and loves us. Brothers and sisters, do not gild your hearts with the pretext of being Christian. Do not gild it with dogmas and ceremonies, with theological phrases about how God must be. Experience Christ in you! He lets Himself be found in us.

Let us give thanks for the Ten Commandments and the Sermon on the Mount, by fulfilling them step by step. Then the love for God and neighbor grows and we become conscious brothers and sisters to one another, as Christ wants it to be. Let us thank Christ that as a carpenter He showed us that we need nothing but a filled heart, the treasure of the inner being, in order to find the way out of our entanglements, out of the network that we have spun ourselves into, like the spider that waits to devour its victim.

Christ is present in us. Let us begin with ourselves to no longer nail Him to the cross again and again, that is, to sacrifice Him through our sins. Let us go to Christ in us. Then the inner tabernacle opens and we find our way to our origin, which is God in us, and we in Him. And then we unearth the treasure of the love for God and neighbor and consciously be brothers and sisters, beyond all borders. Then Christ is risen in us.

The one who lets Christ rise in him is a brother, a sister; he does not need "honors"—he honors solely the One who is worthy of all honor. Through his Redeemer-deed, Christ has chosen each one of us. When we choose Him as the center in our lives, then we will honor Him, praise and glorify Him, love Him and do what He asked of us as Jesus of Nazareth: *Follow Me.*

A nameless one, with the name Gabriele, merely to identify herself in this world, a follower of Jesus, of Christ, asks her brothers and sisters: Let us follow Him—and there will be peace.

Peace
Gabriele

Influencing and manipulating
our neighbor by
projecting our correspondences

The law of correspondence conforms to the person who has entered it into himself through his sinful way of thinking, speaking and acting. Every person has programmed and programs his conscious mind and subconscious, as well as his soul, with his feeling, thinking, speaking and acting. The result is a human personality that consists of the programs for a life on Earth and its processes, the programs of perception for an earthly life and the programs of sin which, in turn, correspond to the person.

Every individual lives, acts and works with the programs of perception that determine the course of our daily life, and with our correspondences, the sins. Seen as a whole, the programs of perception and of correspondence form the present state of consciousness of the person. Part of this is also that part of the consciousness that has been opened again, the already free part of the soul.

The law of correspondence of one person is not the law of correspondence of another. Every one feels, thinks, speaks and acts according to his specific laws of perception and of correspondence, according to his own state of consciousness. This is what he works with and what he uses to influence others in many ways, in order to project his correspondence, his opinion, into them. The projections of correspondences from one person into another often take place deviously or with purposeful pressure, so that the other accept the correspondence, the opinion, of the one.

When a person successfully insinuates his opinion into the mind of another by projecting it into him, he can control the one upon whom he has imposed a part of his correspondence; because, with his successful programming, a channel was established for influencing the other person. The one who has influenced, that is, programmed, the other by clever insinuation, has then become a part of the other in terms of his burdening potential.

In this way, the law of correspondence becomes the law of projection: What corresponded to the one, now, through insinuation, also corresponds in part to the other. Formulated on a personal level: What corresponded to me, now, by way of insinuation, corresponds to you. The programming, that is, manipulation, was successful. My correspondence became a projection. I have entered my way of thinking, my idea, into my neighbor. Consequently, my character—and thus, a part of my fate—has become interwoven with that of my neighbor, for this process was also entered as an input into the repository planets of the Fall-cosmos.

Every person is an extensive memory bank, which is connected with the causal memory bank of the material cosmos and with that of the purification planes through his personal, human, that is, earthly and sinful, inputs. But as human beings we are also, and will always be, the child of God. The heart of every soul in a human being is the incorruptible core of being, God, which links soul and person with the eternal Being, the eternal law.

Through this core of being, God, everything pure is in communication with the pure. The impure of each individual, his sinfulness, communicates, in turn, with the sinfulness that is stored in his soul and in the causal network of entanglements. Based on the principle "like attracts like," the pure communicates with the pure, and the impure, with the impure.

The mixing board of programs.
The computer "human being" veils
his true intentions

The human being can be compared to a computer. It is known that a computer can print out only what has been entered in it, that is, what has been stored in it. It is similar with the computer "human being." A person can express only what he has entered into himself, that is, what is stored in him. With a technical computer one does not speak of correspondences, because it prints out unaltered the data that has been entered into it, unless there is a so-called virus in the computer system, through which false information can develop or programs can even be destroyed.

The computer "human being," who has programmed himself, has more possibilities to express himself than does a technical computer. He is able to mix parts of his programs. Thus, the computer system "human" can be compared to a mixing board: The mixed programs, the tools of the human art of self-display, of covering up and of deceit, often consist of glossed over words and actions.

Consequently, it may be that the computer "human being" can pass on only what he has stored like a technical computer, but beyond that, he is capable of preparing a mixture from parts of his programs, by presenting facts and things not as they are, but embellished and colored. In addition, he is able to project his correspondences into his fellow people, in order to manipulate them, that is, to misuse them for his own purposes.

Therefore, the individual can color and embellish his correspondences, his emotions like anger, hate, envy, as well as his opinions, concepts and intentions. This means that he can resourcefully and purposefully modify them to make them more palatable to his neighbor, so that the latter take in this mixture and let himself be programmed, and thus, influenced and manipulated.

Here is an example of such a mixture:

An employee envies the promotion of a colleague at work, which includes a corresponding raise in salary. The mixture that develops from his correspondence, envy, may be formulated as follows: "This overachiever worked overtime without pay; he bowed and scraped before the boss for so long, until his attention was drawn to the seemingly competent worker. But I," so thinks the colleague who is green with envy, "will see to it that things don't go well very long for him in his new position. I will uncover every mistake he makes and expose his weaknesses."

This is how the person filled with envy thinks, but his mixture sounds different. To his ex-colleague he speaks honeyed words, "You deserve this promotion, because you have rendered outstanding service to the firm. If you ever need help or have any kind of trouble, feel free to come to me. I will always find time to help you. I wish you all the best in your new job, with friendly and helpful colleagues."

From where does the envy-filled colleague take his words, which not only color his thought-program, his correspondence, but even dress up his envy with declarations of favor and offers to help, beautifying his correspondence, the feelings of envy, with chocolate icing, as it were? The aspects which beautify his envy, the chocolate icing, he takes from parts of the world of his programs—for example, from the world of his desires—because speaking with a forked tongue can, in all its aspects, variations and forms of expression, come only from the computer "human being."

How did the mixing board of programs develop? The pure spirit being from which the human being came forth, knows no deception, no forked tongue. A being of the heavens *is*. What it is, the law, God, is what it radiates and that is what it "expresses," what it does and what it moves in. A spirit being is the truth and is in the truth. It is truthful; its deed is the same as its word, and its word is the same as its divine sensing.

The pure expresses itself directly and genuinely. Ambiguity, which comes from deception, a forked tongue, emerged with the Fall. The first

Fall-being wanted to hide its divergent sensations from the divine; as a result, thoughts developed. Thus, we could call this Fall-thought the first non-divine thought. We recognize that the Fall was not only a falling away from God, but also a fall from being one-in-itself. A kind of divisiveness resulted. The Fall-beings built their false bottom, this "double tongue," namely, their world of thoughts, which was different than what their sensations and feelings indicated. When the spoken word, the human language, was added to this, the "third bottom," as it were, the "third tongue" became manifest.

Therefore, we can say that the mixing board of programs developed because the human being thinks other than he senses and feels, and speaks other than he thinks and feels, but also acts other than he speaks, thinks, senses and feels. Countless variations are possible from his colorful repertoire of feelings, sensations, thoughts, words and actions. Depending on his momentary intentions, a person puts together the corresponding combination for his way of speaking or acting.

Back to our example:

If the one who has climbed to a higher position now accepts the flattering words of his former colleague as being sincere and makes use of what was offered to him, that is, if he again and again turns to his former colleague with questions and worries, then the latter has succeeded in projecting his own correspondences into him. The promoted person, who has taken some steps on the ladder to success, who has "swallowed" the mixture and carries parts of the correspondences of his former colleague in him—his ambition, his striving for success and envy—will think of him right away when he cannot manage a task or when he has other worries. In the good faith that he will receive help and solutions from him, he reports his difficulties and problems to this person, whom he seemingly can trust—but who in reality only wants to spy on him. His former colleague, however, who offered him his help in a nicely colored, that is, hypocritical, way, abuses his trust, wanting to harm him.

This is only one example of the countless intrigues that are produced on the mixing board of the world of programs of the individual. Similar things happen every day at the enterprises and establishments of this world.

This example can be used for all the spheres of our life, for the thinking, speaking and acting of the most influential authority all the way to the school child who envies his fellow pupil for his carefully formed sandcastle and tramples it, saying, "We are not supposed to build any castles" or "Your castle doesn't have a moat around it." In this school child, envy has already turned color. An apparently positive statement that sounds helpful and kind bears envy in it.

*Our correspondences, our sins, our inputs
are our character and our fate—
as are the programs from our projections*

As explained, a technical computer produces what has been entered in it. It does not arbitrarily mix the programs. It also doesn't present itself in a different light than what it is, based on its memory bank; nor will it try to deceive in any way the computer expert or whoever works with it. Here, the question comes up as to whether a technical computer isn't actually a better colleague than the computer "human being," who puts his mixing board to work, as it were, and produces what will be advantageous to him?

A computer has its color and shape, its discs, its memory bank, its operating system and its files, which it can refer back to at any given moment. With what is in it, it can communicate with other computers through cable or telephone. Through different input systems, it can take in new data or change existing ones—but always only within the framework of the existing programs and the stored data. Normally, it will never initiate on its own totally new actions that were not intended as a program.

The computer "human being" has his own form, also according to the data stored in his memory bank. The correspondence programs of a person can be compared with tools like a chisel or a paintbrush. Just as a sculptor chips out a sculpture from a stone with a chisel, so is the shape of a person's body formed by his feeling and thinking. Just as the paintbrush or pencil of an artist draws a picture stroke by stroke, so does a person draw his physical body with his correspondences, with his human way of feeling, thinking, speaking and acting.

This takes place at every moment, because we feel, sense, think, speak and act at every moment. As a result of this, our radiation changes minute by minute. We are what goes out from us. Thus, the individual shapes his life and his surroundings—and as he is, he has a direct or indirect effect on his neighbor.

What and how we are, what and how we express ourselves, what and how we act, everything that is not divine is stored in the Fall-cosmos— unless we recognize it beforehand and delete it by clearing it up. Thus, every person is marked by the data he has entered into his memory. What he stored yesterday can be his today and his today can be his tomorrow.

A proverb says, "Every person is the architect of his own fate." One person bears many sinful inputs; his soul, as well as his conscious mind and subconscious, are heavily burdened. As a result, his soul and body have a low vibration. With this vibration, he then affects his environment. On the other hand, another person turns more and more to the divine, by recognizing his sinfulness, repenting and clearing it up, no longer committing it and fulfilling the laws of God step by step. This person, too, is marked by his thinking and acting; soul and physical body vibrate more highly, because higher forces are radiating through them. He emits positive radiation, positive thoughts that reach those people who are searching and striving for the truth.

Our stored correspondences, our sins, are the engravings of our physical body. We either bear the light of our soul or we display the shadows of our soul, the sins. Each one of us is the identification card of his inner being, of what corresponds to him, what he himself has input. That is our character.

If we allow second, third or fourth persons to plant into our minds their concepts and desires, if we take in the projections of our neighbor, this is possible only because similar aspects are already stored in our soul or in our subconscious or conscious mind. These already existing engrams form the basis, the magnets, as it were, which attract the same and like things. We could also express it in the following way: The seed of the one falls onto the fertile soil of the other.

When we take the projections of others into the repertoire of our own programs, of our correspondences, then we have expanded the world of our programs. By taking over parts of the programs of others, we are, at the same time, bound to them.

The law of correspondence can also be called the law of transmission. In what way?

We people have the habit of thinking at great length about negative things. For example, if one person hates another, he will then brood for a long time about how he can express his malice toward the other. A physical law states that no energy is ever lost.

As an illustration, the following picture: We can compare a negative thought with a wasp that carries its "poison" in itself. Thus, a person who broods and ponders is surrounded by a whole swarm of "wasps" that move around aggressively. The hot-tempered, hate-filled thoughts of the one swarm about in the atmosphere like a swarm of wasps, seeking their like. They may not even end up landing on the person who is hated by the other one, but will land wherever they find what "corresponds" to them—the same or like milieu, the same or like world of feelings and thoughts.

Once the "wasps," these vagabond thoughts, have found identically or similarly vibrating inputs in a person, they then sting him, so as to "inject" their poison into the corresponding program of their victim. Their "victim," who already has the same kind of energies in him—feelings or thoughts of hatred—gets even more upset. The poison of the first one enflames the emotions of his fellow person, whom he may not even know, ever more, until the latter finally goes into action, thus becoming a wrongdoer, whom our courts call to account and, if applicable, pass sentence on. The culprit is punished. But the instigator, who had emitted his brooding, hate-filled thoughts, thus contributing to the fact that the other became a criminal, walks around apparently free.

According to the law of cause and effect, the instigator is bound to the culprit. He may not even know him, but the entanglements in the causal network will one day reveal what lies between them. The "sun" will bring these debts to light; either from the effects or from the results, we will recognize that we have burdened ourselves and have built up a karmic thread, a binding.

Therefore, we can transmit to others our emotion-laden thoughts. We also call this telepathy. Often, one thought that went out from us is the spark that sets off the explosion in a "powder keg," the last impetus that leads our neighbor to commit a crime, perhaps turning him into a criminal. For this deed and for everything that results from it, we bear a part of the guilt.

We can recognize the simple teaching of Jesus of Nazareth, of the Christ of God, who said and says, "What the person sows, he will reap"—unless he recognizes his causes in good time, in order to clear them up with the power of Christ and no longer commit them.

If we think about these brief explanations in all their consequences, many will surely say, "This is outrageous," or even, "This is horrible." Both are true; due to the principle of "sending and receiving," much is possible. Through the projections that we allow others to insinuate in us, or that are transmitted to us through telepathy, because we have the same or like correspondences in us, we adopt a part of the character of others, to whom, for example, we are servile. We let ourselves be programmed and manipulated.

The web of the spider is its world. Like a spider, we people spin our web, the web of our correspondences, of our programs. This is what we live in; it is our ego world and we are caught in it—and through the threads of our projections we are also tied to the network of our neighbor.

But the principle of "sending and receiving" is also effective in a positive sense.

If we send out positive, peaceful, unifying thoughts, then these also pass on their inherent message. For example, they can be picked up by a person who is considering the possibility of committing murder. Our positive flying thoughts may find entry into the considerations of "for and against" of the negative thinker. The scale of his heart is tipped by the positive energies of our thoughts; the waves of his hatred are quieted; his reason and conscience gain the upper hand. If we can thus prevent our fellow person, whom we don't even know, from committing a terrible act, we become the liberator and unknown friend—without our or their being aware of it—of the one who refrained from committing the deed and whose life may now turn toward the good.

Protection from influence:
Recognize yourself; attain steadfastness
in Christ, and turn to the positive forces.
"What you do not want others
to do to you ... "

Many will wonder "How can I protect myself against the influences, against the projections of others or even against telepathic transmissions?"

There is only one protection: Learn to know yourself, your behavior, your character, which consists of your personal feelings, sensations, thoughts, words and actions. With the help of the Christ of God, clear up daily the sinfulness that today shows you, and do not commit this sin anymore. In this way, you attain steadfastness in Christ and no longer let yourself be influenced by the desires, passions, opinions and concepts of your fellow people. Once we have found our hold in the divine Self, we will no longer lean on anyone or imitate others.

If we change ourselves in this way, then our character changes, and with this, the appearance of our body as well. Thus, many who are bent over begin to straighten up when they turn to the positive powers. Many a wrinkle disappears when a person begins to feel and think in a positive way more and more, when he affirms the positive powers in everyone and in everything, and sets out to develop them.

Daily, we influence our character through the impressions we take in via our senses, via our feelings and our way of thinking and speaking. Our character, in turn, marks our physical body.

If we do not think this is possible, then a mirror, in which we can observe the image of our external appearance, can give us a good "reading." Let us look into a mirror, especially when something moves us, when we are happy or depressed, hateful or envious! We can read a lot about ourselves in our reflection. Through this, we directly experience our character portrait, which is new every day, depending on the situations that the day brings and also on our daily way of feeling, thinking, speaking and acting, that is, our daily new programming.

If we want to shape our life in a positive way, if we want a pure character, an open nature, we can begin to practice being of good will. What helps us with this is the spiritual principle that says, "What you do not want others to do to you, do not do it to others either."

Each one of us wants to be understood and accepted by others. Each one of us wants our neighbor to think positively and kindly of us. Therefore, let us first practice kindliness ourselves! This does not mean that we should flatter our neighbor, but that we should affirm the good in him, for the good is found in every person, since God, the all-knowing love and wisdom, is in the soul of every person and in every cell of his physical body as well. If we practice being one with our fellow people instead of separating ourselves from them, we will become kinder, more understanding and of good will. Understanding, good will and kindness lead us to see and understand our neighbor in the right way.

Let us also practice freedom by no longer binding our neighbor to ourselves through our projections when we want to win him over to our desires or our way of thinking. If we leave him freedom in his thinking, speaking and doing, then we become tolerant. Tolerance gradually leads to unity with our neighbor.

A person who disciplines himself in order to drive out his own falseness also learns to recognize his neighbor better and to see him in the right light. If we tighten the reins on ourselves in order to discard our own vices, then we also learn to understand our neighbors and find inner unity with them.

Jesus said in the following sense, "Why do you see the splinter in your brother's eye and do not perceive the beam in your own eye?"

If we first work on the beam in our own eye, then we also have the strength to speak with our fellow person about the splinter in his eye, without becoming teachy, offensive or intolerant.

A person who watches and examines and monitors himself and keeps telling himself again and again, "What I do not want others to do to me I will not do to them" will remove the beam from his own eye through this self-discipline. In this way, he takes the steps that bring him closer to his neighbor, and with good will, understanding and kindness, he learns how to see and understand his fellow people in the right way. Then it will no longer be difficult for him to leave each one their freedom and to be tolerant toward all.

In this way, the basis is formed for gaining respect for his fellow people. The person who respects his neighbor will also honor God, the eternal love, more and more, by fulfilling step by step the purpose for which he is on Earth: to keep the commandments of God.

All changes toward the good, toward the divine in us transform our character; we become nobler. From an upright character, an honest person develops who values his fellow people, because he changes himself instead of wanting to change his neighbor.

The love for God and neighbor grows in the person who honors God in his character traits, and in his whole world of thinking. Such people stand with their feet firmly on the ground. They are steadfast, clear, upright and honest. They are the ones who are able to find answers and solutions in difficult situations and to turn everything toward the good.

*The character, behavior and
body structure of a person are formed
by his feelings, sensations, thoughts,
words and actions.
Programs that we set up today are
components for future incarnations*

By changing toward the good, we learn to look deeper. People can blind and deceive us only as long as we blind and deceive ourselves. Once we have developed an upright character, we are often able to look into the hidden aspects of our fellow people and to see them as they really are. We may well see the faults and weaknesses of our fellow people, but we do not judge or condemn.

As already stated, it can be read on every person what they really are. The markings of an individual are formed in manifold ways, depending on their positive and negative programs. We change every day, every hour anew, according to our patterns of behavior. We move and behave according to our markings.

Nothing happens by chance. The whole person draws his own markings from the top of his head to the soles of his feet. Down to the tiniest details, the smallest dimples and wrinkles, everything was entered by the individual himself into his soul and into his genes.

Therefore, it is not by chance that we have this particular body structure; each one has his own specific body structure that is subject to his character. It is not by chance that one person has this hair color and someone else another, that our hairline is higher or lower, that our forehead is wider or narrower. Whether a person has his hair parted or not, whether the part falls to the right or to the left or in the middle—everything lies in his character. It is not by chance, for example, that someone's hair is thick or thin or falls out, totally or partly. Even his hairstyle is not by chance. It is not by chance that a nose is long or short, bent or straight, that a person has prominent cheekbones, or eyes that are widely or closely spaced.

His eyebrows as well, and the color of his eyes, the color of his face and his features all result from his genes and from his character. The shape of his ears and nose, the small and deep wrinkles in his face are not by chance. The flat or prominent, wide, pointed or dimpled chin alone says a lot about the character of a person.

All of this is drawn by the brush of our countless feelings, sensations, thoughts, words and actions, our passions, longings, desires and the like. Our character traits, our character sketches, that mark us have for the most part been entered by us into our soul, and through this, into our genes in previous incarnations. A person who knows about reincarnation knows that nothing happens by chance.

All of infinity is law. The same is true for the world of our programs—all that we have entered into our consciousness and subconscious, into our soul and the repository planets. It is our personality law that takes its course in rhythms and cycles, which marks and influences us.

Our programming affects the smallest components of our body. No two people have the same hands. Every hand is different and has its own detailed markings; every one marked it himself through his own programming during this life or in earlier lives. It is not by chance that one person has straight and another one sloping shoulders or that his shoulders are wide or narrow. Whether our arms are long or short, whether our waist and hips are narrow or broad, whether our torso is large or delicate, whether we have bowed or straight legs—even the size of our shoes is something we ourselves have determined through our own programming. Whether our gait is upright or bent over, whether we take large or small steps, we ourselves have determined this through our inputs, which, at the same time, are specifications for our body.

Every skin pigment wants to tell us something; our teeth speak to us; our fingernails and toenails have their language. The person who has learned to perceive, who has recognized himself and overcome his sinfulness reads the external aspects of a person like an open book.

Everything, absolutely everything, is our own personal expression. Our movements, our gestures and facial expressions, the expression of our mouth, every little wrinkle on our body, every freckle—everything was determined by ourselves, by the individual traits of our character, which mark and imprint our body as well as our fate. Even the forms and colors of the clothes we choose, the shape of the shoes we have worn, the furnishings of our home and how we live in it, the surroundings in which we live as well, our tastes, our habits—all of this we have determined ourselves. The way we sit on a stool or in an armchair, the way we lie in our bed corresponds to our programming. Every step was predetermined by ourselves. All our thinking, speaking and acting comes from the world of our own programs, of our character. Everything, but everything, is the imprinting we made—and no one else.

The food or drink we take, how we prepare our food, the way we eat and hold our spoon, fork or knife in our hand and the way we raise a glass of liquid to our mouth—all of this is in our character portrait; it draws our body and determines our behavior.

Today, seen as a whole, we cannot change the structure of our body that we have created in previous incarnations. But we can give ourselves a different radiation, a radiation frequency that vibrates on a higher or lower level. This, in turn, takes place through our five senses, which imprint us via our feeling, thinking, speaking and acting, as well as via the world of our desires. We can change our behavior, which corresponds to our inner attitude, our character, by either refining it or making it more coarse. And so, partial aspects—like the form and color of our clothes, our eating habits, our gestures and facial expressions, our gait, our way of speaking—can change, but not the basic structure of our body.

Every day, we draw ourselves anew, and each day we predetermine a corresponding character sketch, which then has an indirect influence on our present physical body. Once the material body has passed away and the soul incarnates again in the cycle of incarnation that it has determined for itself, then the data that we have entered today into our soul and into the cosmos of the purification planes, as well as into the material cosmos, can find direct expression tomorrow, that is, in the next incarnation. What we enter into the soul and into the genes today, in this incarnation, is what we can be tomorrow, in another form of existence—if the inputs of today are fully active in the stars, in the soul and in the genes.

If we were to die today, the inputs for tomorrow, for another sojourn on Earth, or for the path as soul in the spheres of purification, would be ready. We are connected to the computer of the material cosmos and of the purification planes through these countless inputs, that is, programs in our soul and in our body. The radiation of the repository stars in this cosmos shows us daily the programs that are active in us today and that we should recognize, analyze and clear up.

No person is left helplessly at the mercy
of his inputs, his correspondences,
programs and their effects.
Recognize yourself!
Your conscience admonishes you

Again and again, we hear: God in us. What is meant is the incorruptible core of being, God, the love that dwells in every soul. Through the divine in us, the incorruptible core of being, we are in direct communication with the eternally pure worlds of the heavens, the eternal Being. On the other hand, through our sinfulness, the burdens of our soul, we are in communication with those stars in the purification planes that have stored our sinfulness. These are then the pathways, the energetic pathways that lead the soul into the spheres beyond and perhaps from there, into this side of life again.

Our physical body, which consists of earth and water, is also connected to the material cosmos that introduces the process of decomposition after physical death, accompanies the conversion process of the human shell into water and earth, and also keeps stored the programs of our previous life on Earth, which then serve us as presettings, so to speak, for a further incarnation.

However, no person is irrevocably left at the mercy of his own inputs, his programs, that is, his correspondences. If he is alert every day and examines his world of feelings and thoughts, his words, actions and passions, he can recognize his own character from this and remedy the negative imprinting.

The basic principle in exploring who we really are is: Recognize yourself. There are many mirrors for this. Our faults and weaknesses, our burdens, are reflected in and on our body and our face, in our family, in relatives, friends, colleagues and managers; there are also the mirror effects of those whom we pass on the street, with everything that they set into motion in us. Our behavior while eating and drinking is also a mirror for us, as well as our sitting posture, our clothing, its form and color, also the furnishings, the colors and forms of our home, our surroundings—everything is a mirror for us.

We could also call the law of correspondence the "law of mirrors." For the person who wants to recognize himself in order to overcome his human aspects and become free, the encounters and experiences with his own reflections are an inestimable help.

There are many more mirrors that help us recognize ourselves, for example, our behavior when we think we are unobserved or are being observed by others. The situations in traffic can also be a mirror for us, for example, when another car passes us illegally, or when a car comes too close to our vehicle. How we park our car or bicycle, how we behave at the checkout counter in a department store—all of these are mirrors for us. Everything, absolutely everything, speaks to us. Our actions and their resulting behavior want to say something to us, not to our neighbor.

Through all these and countless other external signs, we reveal our true character, that is, the programs that mark and control us. All these different character traits are the crayons that give our body its characteristic expression. Even the way we express ourselves when we speak, our choice of words, the emphasis we place on our words, the sound of our voice, our thinking, but also our world of feelings, are all expressions of the inputs that have been stored in our soul, in our conscious mind and subconscious, that is, they are expressions of our character. Whether we determine our neighbor, suggesting our ideas to him, by projecting our correspondences into him, or transmitting telepathically our strong egocentric thoughts to him—or whether we leave him his freedom in his thinking and acting, all these are a part of our personal inputs, which mark us.

The sum of all the programs in our soul and in our conscious mind and subconscious make up our state of consciousness. What we are is what we radiate, and that, in turn, radiates back toward us from everything. Unceasingly, we receive impulses from our own inputs in the repository stars of the Fall-cosmos, according to the principle of "sending and receiving."

The incorruptible core of being, God, the good in us, also emits signals unceasingly. In addition to other divine help by way of guardian beings from the eternal Being, these impulses form our conscience. We feel pangs of conscience with every non-divine stirring and inclination in us, for example, with aggressions, envy, greed, egotistical acts and the like. Even when we talk nicely, but think impurely, our conscience stirs.

Often, our conscience, which reveals itself through the most subtle layers of our plane of feelings, first makes itself felt in our solar plexus. There, we feel a sense of unease, which is like a slight queasy feeling. If we go after these most subtle signals by exploring the world of our feelings, we open a door, so to speak, through which the impulses flow from the core of being, from God and the guardian beings, into the world of our thoughts. In our rising thoughts, we can then read what our conscience is signaling to us.

But the person who deadens his conscience—by basically keeping to his egotistical attitude—will in time lose his conscience. He covers it up with many layers of his own egoism, and because of this, has hardly any access to his feelings. A person who has lost his conscience has also lost his character. He is without conscience or character and concerned only with his ego, his base self. This, too, marks a person. He is then the expression of his lack of character.

*Everything is the law—either divine
law or the law of our ego.
Like attracts like*

The one who reads this book attentively and examines himself will immerse into the yet unknown depths of the world of his senses, of his stirrings and inclinations. Only then, does our life become truly interesting, because the person who becomes an explorer of his own base self also finds access to the deepest programs that he created in his previous lives and that influence his present life on Earth. Whoever takes a plain and honest look at himself in the mirror of facts will gradually realize that every person creates his own law and that his personal principles emerge from his personal inputs, from his feeling, thinking, speaking and acting, that is, from his whole behavior.

The seed—which consists of the world of our senses, of our way of feeling, thinking and acting and that we sow into the acre of our soul—will be our harvest. If we sow good seed, we will reap a good harvest. If we sow bad seed, then we will have a bad harvest. Discord, discontent, selfishness, passions, hatred, envy, animosity, greed and much more are our ego; they are the aspects that form our fate. They are the harvest of our sowing.

Many of us ask again and again, "What will fate bring to me and my own?" And many a one thinks that our fate lies hidden in a fog of the incomprehensible. But this isn't so. Many things become evident to us when we take a look into our world of thoughts, into our whole behavior. A person who explores only on the surface will easily deceive himself. We have to understand the expressions of our life in their depth; we have to get to the bottom of them.

Thoughts and words, for example, are like shells that bring across something different than what their contents are. Especially the contents of the shell—that is, what lies behind the thoughts, words and deeds, for example, the motivation, the contents of the feelings, the true intentions— all these are aspects of inputs that determine our fate, and are often already signs of the outbreak of a blow of fate.

In the contents of our thoughts, words and actions, we can read the aspects of the different fates that we have engraved. *When* these will come into effect is determined by the action of the stars in which our inputs are stored. *Whether* this particular fate comes into effect is determined by each one of us himself. Christ comes several steps toward the one who repents of the sins he has recognized each day with the power of the Christ of God, clears them up and no longer commits them. Christ also erases many a blow of fate in him. He transforms the perilous negativity into positive life force, into the power of love and of mercy.

Everything that surrounds us, what we see and what we cannot perceive with our physical eyes is the law. Whether it is the orbits of the stars, gravitation, the processes in the nature kingdoms, the behavior of our neighbor or whether we are thinking about our own actions—we meet the principles of the law everywhere. Whether we move here or there, whether we choose this or that travel route, whether we travel to this or that country, whether we travel by airplane, by ship, by car or by train, everything has already been determined in us. These inputs are like control mechanisms. They are the tools of the stars in which, as already explained, our inputs are registered. They affect the world of programs of our soul and the conscious mind and subconscious of our physical body as well. They bring our character into movement and mark our body.

It is important for each one of us to differentiate between the law of God, the law of love and peace, on one hand, and the law of our ego, on the other.

Our immortal spiritual body consists of the countless spiritual principles of the eternal law, God. From this all-encompassing law of love and wisdom, we received the Ten Commandments through Moses and the Sermon on the Mount from Jesus, the Christ. These spiritual principles are meant to be commandments of guidance for us, which we can use as orientation, in order to find our way into the all-encompassing eternal law of God, the love. From the love, from God, stream freedom, joy, happiness, harmony, equality, unity and justice. The pure spirit body is, therefore, the essence of all that is pure in infinity.

The law that relates to the person, to the "human aspects" of the person, is the law of the personal ego. It consists of the programs, the correspondences, of the individual, of the personal, egotistical principles of the law that relate to our small world, the world of our ego. These law principles of our ego, which we have created ourselves, overlay the divine in us. We work with these program inputs. They are, figuratively speaking, our tools. With them, we influence our neighbor and our environment.

The principle of the law of infinity "like draws to like" or "like attracts like" also holds true for our correspondences. We attract back to us the same or similar things that we emit from our human, sinful programs, what we instigate and do with them. They will befall and control us.

According to the law of sending and receiving, of like attracts like, only what we have sent out comes back to us again. Pure beings attract only the pure, because they fulfill the pure, the divine law. The impure being, the human being, often attracts the impure that he has entered into himself, which marks him, the person. As long as we create correspondences for ourselves, we also create and expand the world of our personal laws that are our own echo, for what we send out is what we receive.

By transforming our ego-law and
fulfilling the laws of God, we create
a luminous picture of our existence
and draw closer to the image of God.
Our personal communications network
emerges with the projection of
mixed programs of correspondence

The law of God consists of the seven basic powers, Order, Will, Wisdom, Earnestness, Patience, which is kindness, Love and Mercy, which is meekness.

The egotistical law that each individual personally created and still creates consists of disorder, self-will, intellectual striving, of carelessness, impatience, self-love, which is self-interest, and mercilessness, which is ruthlessness.

With the turning away of the Fall-beings and the continuous sinning of human beings, the seven divine basic powers, the law of God, were reversed to become the seven egotistical forces of creation that are the human ego. With these seven egotistical forces, every person creates his sins and his share in the global karma, the world-guilt. This is his egotistical heritage. The individual inputs are the human character, the personal aspects of each individual; these cannot be relegated to others. This individual law is our work volume. We draw from it and with it, we influence our neighbor and our environment.

We can also view our correspondences as a workbench on which we chisel and hammer out more programs, like, for instance, the programs of cunning and trickery to gain our own advantage. The workbench of our correspondences also serves us to twist the programs we have produced in such a way that provides them with seemingly logical arguments, to embellish them with suggestions that take the weaknesses of our neighbor into consideration, so that he fall for them and we can easily project our programs into him, that is, insinuate them in him.

The person who does not examine himself and forge himself into shape, by working on his sinfulness and turning it into God-pleasing thinking and acting, will one day be forged by his neighbors, who then insinuate their way of thinking, their wanting and desires in him, by projecting them into him or by transmitting them to him through telepathy.

Since God dwells in every person, each person has in himself the help and strength of the Christ of God to transform his correspondences, that is, his sinfulness, so that from his individual law, his ego-law, he find his way into the law of God. Thus, every person is called to bring the seven basic powers of God, which each individual has reversed in different ways, into balance again: from disorder to Order, from self-will to the Will of God, from intellectual striving to divine Wisdom, from carelessness to Earnestness, from impatience to Patience, from self-love, which is self-interest, to Love for God, from mercilessness, which is ruthlessness, to Mercy.

The law of God is immutable. At some point in time, we have to transform our ego-law and fulfill the spiritual principles of God, for the law of the Eternal is absolute, irrevocable. Either we change, and through this, again become loving, peaceful, healthy, joyful, happy and God-conscious, or we continue to build on our ego, on the law of correspondence, and will continue to reap what we have sown or created, so to speak.

If we continue to sow hatred and envy, then we will be hit with hatred and envy. If we continue to sow discord and quarreling, we will be faced with the same or like thing; if we sow enmity and others have to suffer because of us, then we will attract the same or something similar to ourselves.

The character that we have drawn of ourselves is registered in many different ways—as was explained. The whole complex of our inputs forms our personal communications network. Thus, the person is the spider that has spun its web, and he is the one who is being pulled by the threads of the web.

The energetic "threads" of this web go out from us to our fellow people, to places, to things, to life forms, but also to discarnate souls, to repository planets in the material cosmos and to repository planets in the purification planes. Our inputs in the repository stars of the Fall-cosmos with their counterpart in the inputs, in the programs in our soul, in our brain cells, in our genes and in all the cells of our body, determine our fate.

If parts of our same or like inputs from the different stars amass and collectively influence us, like beads strung together, so to speak, then parts of our own programs in us will connect, and then affect our body more strongly, triggering illness, blows of fate, hardship and the like.

Each one of us inputs today what will be tomorrow or what will befall him tomorrow. Our behavior is decisive. Either we turn to God and develop a light-filled, noble character, a luminous picture of our life that approaches the divine image, or we continue to develop our egotistical image, which identifies itself as a bad character and presents itself in form and shape, showing who our person really is.

If we want to recognize ourselves, we should look into the many mirrors with which we are confronted daily: our fellow people and the many situations of the day. They reflect our divine behavior or our correspondences.

The one who begins to practice self-recognition on the basis of the law of correspondence will often feel rather uncomfortable, because it is easier to simply point to one's neighbor and attribute all evil to him. But soon, he will realize that each one can become free only through self-recognition—thanks to the Christ of God who is our Redeemer and our Liberator through His Redeemer-power.

*Through sin, the human being created
and creates his individual perception.
He sees and hears himself*

As already explained, each one of us is the builder of his own law and his own personified law. However, with the help of the Christ of God in us, each one can change for the good every day. If we turn to the Spirit of the Christ of God in us, our character will become nobler, our senses finer, our thoughts more selfless, our words more honest and our deeds more and more pleasing to God. All our thinking and striving is then directed toward sincerity. We will become just, tolerant, of good will, loving. Our senses will then grasp the positive more and more, because our thinking and striving have become more God-conscious. Then we will also fulfill the words of the Christ of God that say in essence, "Do to others first what you would have them do to you."

If we turn away from God, the law of love, then we reverse the words of the Christ of God and say, "The others should do what I want. Then I will think about whether I will do a little bit of what they want." By turning away from God, our sins, that is, our correspondences, influence the world of our senses more and more, which, in turn, shapes our character. This is done in the following way: The inner eye, which beholds the ruling hand of the Godhead, is overshadowed by sin. Through sin, the human being created and creates his individual perception. Sin always sees, in turn, only itself: the sin.

A person who, for example, envies his affluent fellow people, thus imprints his organ of sight. The eye of envy sees again and again only the affluent, people who are in a better position than he. This immediately produces emotions and thoughts. The person concerned sees himself as the one who always gets the short end of things, whom many others have deprived of most, if not all, worthwhile things and still do so.

The world of an envious person is filled with enviable people. He is frequently astonished and outraged, because through his envy-tinted glasses it seems to him that most people have more than he has, and moreover, so he thinks, undeservedly. If we are filled with envy, then we always see, feel, think and hear what our envy inputs in us.

The more often we think about the affluent and foster our envy, the more numerous become the things we associate with them. The countless moments that produce the thoughts, wishes and feelings imprint our conscious mind and our subconscious, as well as the screen of the eye. The pictures of the thoughts and wishes that we have entered into ourselves are reflected by our eyes. The organ of sight thus imprinted is then our individual way of seeing things, which then is reality for us. The divine impulses of love and virtue are overshadowed by sin, by the bad habit of envy.

Someone who is imprinted by envy listens, for example, to a wealthy person. What happens? His organ of sight, which is already programmed accordingly, now influences his hearing with components of the pictures he has engraved in himself. In this way, what he hears is already predetermined. Under the influence of his sight, the envious person then thinks, "It's all very well for him to talk. He has what I don't have. He lives a pleasant life and has others work for him." He continues to think something like the following, "His words are repugnant. I don't want to hear or see him." What the person who is imprinted by envy hears corresponds to the pictures that already cloud his senses. Components of certain pictures that influence and mark his organ of sight now affect his hearing and program it accordingly.

In this way, the person ends up in the dead-end of his ego. We can no longer see things clearly. Through the sinfulness that dominates us, we lose our sense of reality more and more. In order to find this sense of reality and ourselves again, we should, instead of reproaching our neighbor, find in ourselves the cause of our own human weakness, of our envy, in order to clear it up and no longer do it, and instead, build up our strength in a life of the divine principles of the law.

*The reciprocal imprinting of our senses
and of our feelings, sensations, thoughts,
words and actions shapes our behavior
patterns.
Reactions lead to actions*

In all of infinity there is nothing static. Thus, our sense of sight influences our sense of hearing, and the sense of hearing influences the sense of sight; both influence our senses of smell, taste and touch, and these, in turn, influence our senses of sight and hearing. The pictures of our senses imprint our feelings, our thoughts, words and actions, our desires and passions, which subsequently, influence the pictures of our senses. Thus, our small, personal world develops, our ego world, the world of our desires, also the world of our drives and passions, as well the world of colors, forms, fragrances and sounds that corresponds to the way we are.

It was said that the programs of our senses of sight and hearing influence our sense of smell.

The corresponding components of the visual material of our senses of sight and hearing shape our sense of smell. Thus, a person will be led to those smells that correspond to the control mechanisms of his senses of sight and smell. He begins to prefer certain aromas, food and drink. These preferred smells, the preferred food and drink and the desires and thoughts they evoke shape, in turn, the sense of smell. These different programs of smell, which, at the same time, are control mechanisms for the other senses, have their specific odor, which is eliminated via the glands of the body. The programs stored for the sense of smell and all other programming determine the behavior patterns of the person, his character and his body odor.

Many people know the derogatory expression, "I can't stand the smell of him." A person who feels more deeply into this statement knows why he cannot stand his neighbor's odor, what he takes exception to in him. The body odor of the one awakens a correspondence in the other that is stimulated and activated through the sense of sight and smell, the roots of which, however, may lie in a totally different area. The words, "I can't stand the smell of him" contain a deeper meaning for us, about which the world of our feelings and sensations can give information. Therefore, we have to analyze our statement in order to find the reasons, the causes, why we "can't stand the smell" of our neighbor, that is, why we reject him.

We people tend to overlook such and similar thoughts, without becoming aware of the deeper meaning, that is, without being clear about what it wants to tell us. As long as we do not analyze our emotional turmoil, our negative thoughts, words and actions that always lead to emotional turmoil, in order to find the reasons for such outbursts—which we should then clear up with the help of the Christ of God in us and no longer do—we continue to program our conscious mind and subconscious and soul with our wrongdoing which, in turn, shapes our behavior, and thus, our character. The stars, which carry the information we have stored in them, stimulate segments of our behavior—that is, our sinful programs that are our burdens—in a pre-determined cosmic rhythm, so that we can clear up our wrongdoing in time before it comes into effect in and on our body.

If we simply live through our days without heeding what the day wants to show us, then, one day, such a segment of stimulated correspondences or sins will mark us with illness, suffering, worry, hardship and the like. Then we have to harvest what we have sown.

If we program our senses, for example, our senses of smell, taste and touch, with even more wrongful behavior, this new programming will be influenced by the already present programs of our senses, by the way we think, speak and act, as well as by our passions and longings. Thus, the imprinting of a certain sense brings with it further programming and imprintings.

It may very well be that every human being is a computer, but each computer "human" has its own specific programs. We people often choose the same words for a given thing, yet frequently, each one means something different. We may each have our own vocabulary, yet each person fills the word, the shell, with his own character, with his behavior patterns, with his longings and passions, which are in closest communication with his five senses.

Depending on his programming, one person may favor this particular food and that particular fragrance, another one, in turn, another food or another fragrance. If ten people eat the same food and take the same drink, each one will detect in it his own programmed nuance of taste and fragrance. If an individual is asked about the food or aroma, each one will comment something different, according to his particular programming. Even when two people say the same thing about the taste or aroma of a certain food, each one means something different, because, depending on our already existing inputs, we fill each word with different thoughts and feelings.

The sense of touch, too, is controlled by the already existing programs of the senses of sight, hearing, smell and taste, but also by the world of our feeling, thinking and speaking. Our sense of touch is additionally programmed by what we touch, because countless vibrations cling to all objects. If one or more of these vibrations are like our own inputs, our correspondences, then we enter into communication with them. Through this communication, feelings or thoughts can be awakened by way of our sense of touch that correspond to those vibrations that cling to the object we have touched. These then influence our sense of touch, and we program it with these vibrations.

Every one of us touches a great variety of objects every day and takes the most diverse things into our hands. We often greet each other with a handshake. We turn the doorknob to open a door; we press a doorbell; we hold coins and bills in our hands which are fraught with the vibration of very many and very different characters.

Countless vibrations adhere everywhere, and we often take in those that correspond to the world of our programs, through our sense of touch. In this way, via the direct stimulation of our sense of touch, aspects from programs of other senses can become active, which then influence our feelings, our thinking, speaking and acting, our desires and longings.

We see that everything is connected and interwoven in a great communications network, so that perhaps one aromatic nuance or one thought can bring a large part of this communications network into vibration and activate the same or like correspondence aspects in other sensory organs or in a thought program or in the programming of a feeling. These reactions then become actions in our conscious mind. We begin to behave accordingly. We will then also act accordingly and may do this or that, which, until now, we would not have believed possible.

The character portrait of a know-it-all.
The one who takes in the opinions and
concepts of another becomes a part of him;
both are tied to each other

Every program of the world of our sensing, feeling and thinking is filled with countless pictures. Every aspect of each individual picture emits, influences and controls us.

We already used the example of envy. Envy has different variations and deviations. An envious person is, in its broader sense, a rapacious, greedy person who wants to grab everything that appeals to his sense of sight and touch. As impetuously as he behaves, he reaches for things. He wants to touch everything, try out everything, pull everything to him. Moreover, he often thinks that he knows everything better. And so, he wants to touch everything, in order to judge it according to the criteria of the programs of his senses. In this way, he turns away from the inner perception and creates more and more correspondences, his personal principles.

Every know-it-all is intent on having the other person accept his opinion and see things as he does. If the know-it-all sees that the other person is listening, he often beguiles and flatters him with words. In this way, he tries, deliberately or unconsciously, to insinuate his opinion into his neighbor. If his listener is unstable, if he isn't very sure of himself, he lets himself be influenced by the one with the louder voice. And then the standards of the other one become his own. This is then the projection coming from the correspondences of the other one.

Let it be stated once again: The person who takes in the opinions and conceptions, the world of desires and the egocentricity of his neighbor becomes a part of him. The aspects that were projected then also become active in the one who allowed the standards of the know-it-all to become a part of him.

The same is true when people intentionally want to transmit their thoughts to others or induce them to action. Souls, too, can influence people telepathically if a person's programs of correspondences are similar to those of the soul that is bound to the Earth.

A person stays in this caldron of many-sided influences until, with Christ, he leaves this steaming, bubbling pot of egoistic behavior, the constant refrain of which is: He is bad and I am good. He is the evil-doer; I am the innocent one who has to suffer under him. He is intolerant; I am the tolerant one whose freedom is curtailed. He is full of falsehood; I am the honest one whose uprightness is so poorly rewarded. The other one should do this for me and gain that for me. This person should help me go up the ladder of success and the other one should do the dirty work for me. This person is the villain, and so is he and he and he … and I am the irreproachable one who has to suffer many an injustice …

Let us again make ourselves aware that in those aspects that were implanted in a servile person by transmitting a correspondence, by insinuation, the same as projection, and by telepathy, he becomes a part of the other, just as the other becomes a part of him, in the law of cause and effect, of sowing and reaping.

These threads are tied together much more often than we realize. Whenever we "actually" are of another opinion, but nevertheless say yes; whenever we turn off our common sense or even silence our conscience to make it easier for us to believe and approve of what others serve us up with; whenever we say or do something for the sake of keeping the peace that we would otherwise never say or do on our own—that is when we should be very alert and ask ourselves why we act this way. We can find help for our reorientation in the Ten Commandments, in the teachings of the Sermon on the Mount and in the divine principles of equality, freedom, unity, brotherliness and justice.

If the projections are reciprocal, where one person implants a part of his correspondences in another and vice versa, in the course of time, even the genes of both will be influenced. By such an approaching uniformity, both stick like a bur to the other. They are bound. Considering future incarnations, this means that they will keep coming back together because the same or like things tie them to each other. This is the case with many partnerships on this Earth, for example, but not only here. Projection, dependency, leaning on others and the like are widespread. As long as we are still in the thicket of our ego, we can hardly say that we are free.

*Every person has a share in the destruction
of the Earth, of the nature kingdoms
and of the atmosphere, and he will have
to bear the consequences*

Before we turn to the nature kingdoms, let
us briefly summarize the spiritual principles and processes once more.

At every moment, countless feelings and thoughts chase through our brain. Most of them come from our own programs. With the sending potential of our programs, we also influence our surroundings and call up from there, in turn, whatever corresponds to us, whatever is like us.

The different aspects of the energies, which we have stimulated by emitting into our environment, take on form in our conscious mind as feelings and thoughts. If we move these thoughts for a longer period of time, they multiply exponentially and increase our emitting potential. In this way, we expand the world of programs of our sending and receiving station. At every moment, we can influence our programs; we can increase and intensify them or we can transform them step by step, with the help of the Christ of God, by repenting, clearing them up and no longer doing our negativities, our sinfulness. Every change, be it positive or negative, has its effect in and on us as well as in the stars, where our programs are stored.

Each one of us is registered in several ways. These inputs are constantly in action, because during the moments of our days we have many sensory impressions, which, in turn, result in countless feelings and thoughts that keep the inputs in constant motion, in the positive as well as in the negative sense. With our personal programming, that is, with our correspondences, which are our own personal laws, we also influence our environment, for example, the nature kingdoms, which we change according to our standards, our concepts.

In the same way that we influence our neighbor in a small way, we also do it on a larger scale. The majority of people with the same or similar programs try to subordinate everything and everyone to their standard of values. In this way, they also influence the nature kingdoms and change them, for example, by crossbreeding animals, by the way they keep animals, thus determining how animals should live and behave, by "improving" plants, and now, with genetic changes in plants, animals and human beings. Everything should happen at the discretion of people who are caught up in the delusion that they are the lords of creation. Yet the human being may be able to change the external, material form of the nature kingdoms and influence the worlds of the animals, plants and minerals of the Earth with his own value concepts; he may be able to subjugate the animals, torment them and force his will upon them; but he cannot enter his concepts and values into the course of cosmic events, in which the nature kingdoms—which, in their core, their innermost structure, are spiritual—are included. Nor can he influence the spiritual collectives of the plants and the part-soul currents of the animals.

Whatever an individual person does to the nature kingdoms is entered into his sinful world of programs and thus, also into his inputs stored in the material cosmos as well as in the purification planes. The brutal interventions in the nature kingdoms shape the character of person and mark his body.

Often, it appears as if nature subjugates itself to humankind. But this is deceptive. Once the limit of torment and exploitation has been reached, nature rebels, because it does not take over the programs of the human ego as its own quality of life. Nature does not let itself be manipulated on a permanent basis, that is, it does not let itself be programmed. It is neither subject nor object. It is God's creation.

Many people do not believe in the law of sowing and reaping. They think that if they do not accept this law, it does not exist.

If misfortune befalls us, we often say, "The other one is to blame." But according to the Christian teaching it is, "Why do you look at the splinter in the eye of your brother and do not perceive the beam in your own eye?" Thus, we seldom want to see and analyze our part in an occurrence. Only too readily, do we blame chance, the "other one," or God.

If we look at and analyze the condition of our Earth, then we say, and rightly so, that the reason why nature is almost completely destroyed is because human beings act against the laws of nature.

Human beings interfere in the processes of nature and of the elements with methods that go against the nature kingdoms. If we think, for example, of the many harmful substances that are destroying the lungs of the Earth, the forests, the question arises: How can the Earth breathe, and how can it supply people with air that is rich in oxygen? Who will take in and transform the harmful substances, if the forests can no longer do this?

Regulating river courses, paving over green spaces and much more are all interventions in nature, through which, among others things, the cycle of the organism Earth, which consists of all water systems, is obstructed. Not even the atmosphere can offer the Earth protection anymore, since it has been largely destroyed through the causes of humankind. Where such global offences and their results are concerned, many will agree with the statement that what humankind causes, what it has done to nature, will hit humankind again. Many also realize that every person, every single one of us, has contributed or still contributes to the destruction of the Earth and of the atmosphere and will have to bear the consequences of his share in this.

Thus, with regard to the nature kingdoms, there is insight into the principles of the causal law. In our personal lives, we are generally not prepared to accept so readily the law of cause and effect, of sowing and reaping, and to recognize our own causes in their effects. For when we hear that our personal causes result in our personal effects, we are often outraged and cry out, "That cannot be!" We do not want to accept, for example, that we ourselves are responsible for our illness, that our suffering is the result of our own faulty behavior, or, if a blow of fate hits our family, that we have helped cause it.

Why is this so? The main reason for this is that the knowledge of the law of sowing and reaping and of reincarnation has been banned from the

Christian faith and thought for more than four-teen centuries.

The cup is full.
Reincarnation—The key to
the law of sowing and reaping

L et us have another look at the nature kingdoms. The violation of nature has been
going on for many generations. Until a few years
ago, it seemed as though nature was healthy. But
now, seemingly out of the blue, we realize that the
cup is full. Nature is now bringing in the harvest
of what generations have sown, of what was done
to nature.

Similar things are happening in us human beings. We may have sown our seed generations
ago. That part of it we have not cleared up until
now can become active today, in this incarnation.

Many a one will say, "Reincarnation, I don't believe in that." But for more and more people, reincarnation is, among other things, the key to the
world of their correspondences, to their seed. The
result is the realization that it is not God, the love,
who sends us illness, misery or a blow of fate, but

that we ourselves reap the harvest from the seed we have placed into the acre of our soul.

We human beings very quickly blame our neighbor for the misfortune that befalls us. But if we believe in the causal law, in the law of sowing and reaping, then sooner or later the question comes up: When did I sow this? I cannot remember having thought, said or done this or that in this lifetime that could have led to this blow of fate or to this illness. But if we take a look at the statement "What a person sows, he will reap," the logical conclusion is that at some point in time this seed must have been placed into our soul, which today, in this life, then sprouts as illness, suffering, blows of fate or other things.

From Christ, our Redeemer, we know through His divine prophetic revelation that for the soul in the planes of purification, there is only the expiation of guilt. On the Earth, where the soul has a body, a person can recognize his guilt in good time, in his world of thoughts and feelings. He can repent, clear up and no longer do what is sinful. But if we do not heed our conscience, and if we do not use the energy of the day, then it is quite possible that a part of what we have sown in previous incarnations will sprout in this life. And then we reap.

As a result of this, the Earth, God's school on Earth for His fallen children, is a place of expiation and probation. If we take a closer look, we can see that in the purification planes there is only expiation; on the Earth, in the Earth-school, there is expiation and clearing things up in time. Consequently, to grant reincarnation is an act of God's grace, because the soul can return in order to clear up, with the help of the Christ of God, what it would otherwise have to expiate in the beyond.

Reincarnation is a very logical principle within the law of sowing and reaping. It gives us the key to understanding why one child is born sick and another healthy, why one person has this and another that kind of suffering, why one person is hit by a heavy blow of fate and why another one makes his way fairly well through this earthly life. Reincarnation is an early Christian teaching and thus, a teaching of Jesus of Nazareth, even if there are only a few traces left in the Bible that refer to it.

Once reincarnation could no longer be brought forward as an explanation for the differing conditions of life and fate, many questions remained unanswered. The "mysteries of God" now took the place of plausible and logical truth.

Let us briefly look into the "mysteries of God," which are nothing more than the excuses of institutional churches. Let us become aware that if God were to keep just one secret from us, He would be imperfect, just as we human beings are imperfect. What is it that He cannot tell His children? What is it that they may not know? What is it that they should simply believe? The institutional churches give no answer to these questions. But Jesus, the Christ, gives us the answer, for He said the following, "Seek first the Kingdom of God, and all other things will be given to you."

With this, Jesus revealed to us that we are heirs to the Kingdom of God and not only partial heirs to the eternal kingdom, for He said, "The Kingdom of God is within you." If God had given us as pure beings only parts of His kingdom, then He would have kept the other part for Himself, and this would then be His secret. But God gave to each of His children the essence and the light of the entire divine kingdom. Spoken with our words, He saved not a single nook or cranny for Himself; He kept nothing from us.

But if the kingdom of the inner being is shadowed with sin, so that the person no longer has access to this inner kingdom—unless he dissolves the sins, the shadows, with the help of Christ—then the "mysteries of God" are "secreted" in the dark spots that cover the light of the Kingdom of God in himself. God does not keep secrets from His children, even if the institutional churches think differently. They have already claimed a lot of things, which turned out to be mere opinions, like, for instance, the claim that the sun circles the Earth.

If we circle around the sun, Christ, then we will not need the opinion of the institutional churches, because then the light dawns in us. The logic of reincarnation leads us to recognize that God has no mysteries.

The law of sowing and reaping, as well, is convincing in its logic. Since we have been helplessly vegetating under the yoke of "mysteries" for many centuries, we often have to first familiarize ourselves with these fundamental principles of the law that determine our earthly lives and that are as simple as they are ingenious.

A picture: If we were to sow wheat in our field and another were to harvest the ripe grain, what would we say? "Hey! That's my field, my wheat! I sowed it!" But when it comes to our sinful seed, which we have sown into the acre of our soul, then we often get all worked up and say, "That's the seed of my neighbor. My husband, my wife, my children, my parents, my relatives, are to blame," or even, "God is to blame; God doesn't love me; He is without love."

Frequently, we people are still quite illogical. But as soon as we start taking a look at ourselves and analyze our patterns of thought and behavior, instead of always examining our fellow people under the magnifying glass of our own programs, judging them and often blaming them, we will realize that the law of sowing and reaping is effective and that it enables us to see through ourselves and others with the help of the law of correspondence and to remove the shackles of many a projection and manipulation, some of which are many centuries old.

*Forces that we emit through
our thinking and living become
effective in our fate*

L et us once again make ourselves aware of
the following:

What would we say if one of our acquaintances
were to claim that one seed could sprout for another seed and bear its fruit? We would say that
this is nonsense and out of the question. To anyone, it is totally clear that no seed can sprout for
another seed and bear its fruit. But we can sow
some of our own bad seed into someone else's
acre, if the soil has been prepared for this. However, if someone then says that a person who has
influenced another is guilty of the other's fate,
then the one who claims this gets nothing but a
pitying smile, because many are of the opinion
that they carry no blame for the illness, misery
and fate of their neighbor. They believe that they
have not done anything to anyone.

Really not? Let us ask ourselves:

Were we and are we always pure in our thoughts toward our fellow people?

Were and are our thoughts and words sensitive toward our neighbor?

Do we influence no one, determining that he should do this or that for us, even though we could do it ourselves?

Did and do we not put pressure on certain people to fulfill our will even though they do not want to?

How often did we describe some of our neighbors as stupid, dumb or incompetent, in front of third parties or in our thoughts?

Have we never hated anyone or envied someone for this or that? Have we never spoken hypocritically?

Have we never quarreled or lived in enmity with others?

Have we never disparaged one of our fellow people and perhaps subjugated many a one?

Have we restrained our jealousy toward our fellow people?

Have we never seemed to think positively while we were thinking negatively, that is, were we never hypocritical?

How often were we indifferent toward our neighbor?

Our reader may say, "Who doesn't do these things?" That's true! No one is perfect, but each one of us knows about the commandments of God that say: You shall love your neighbor, that is, not wish him something unpleasant or bad, not even in your thoughts. Another excuse could be, "One can't be so particular about everything. Others say and do things that are much worse, and things are going great for them."

Yes, many are blinded by the false sun of ambition, envy, hatred, and exploitation, of influencing others, all the way to wishing to kill them— and things are going great for them. But when the sun of the ego doesn't shine anymore, because the clouds of the causes draw closer and rain their content down on us, then we are outraged by it, because we are convinced that we did not cause anything like what is hitting us now, let alone to our neighbor.

From physics we know that no energy is ever lost. Our feelings, sensations, thoughts, words and actions, including hatred, envy, enmity, quarreling and much more are energies that do not dissolve. Sooner or later, the forces that we have emitted brew together like thunderclouds. This means that from our inputs in the stars, the same and like inputs join together in their vibration and become active through our soul where the same and like aspects are found. Subsequently, they have their effect in and on our body or on our immediate surroundings. Then we experience the effects of our causes, of our seed. Therefore, it is our seed that sprouts, not someone else's.

Is God just?

ime and again, as already mentioned, the objection is raised that there are people who were bitterly evil their whole life long. They used their fellow people and exploited them, not having anything good to say about them—and yet, things went well for them. They grew old and at the hour of death, they simply fell peacefully asleep. Thus, they passed on into the other world during their sleep. On the other hand, there are people who were caring and good friends their whole life long, who certainly did not burden themselves with such guilt, and yet were plagued with illness and afflicted with blows of fate. And sometimes, at the hour of death, they had to fight a tough battle.

But how accurate is a statement like, "This caring and helpful person did not burden himself with such guilt"? Do we know this for sure? Can we read the thoughts of our fellow people? Can we look into their soul? Do we have insight into their previous incarnations?

Where nothing was sown, one does not expect a harvest. If fate hits us, on the one hand, it becomes clear that we caused something, that we have sown something. On the other hand, from the type of occurrence and circumstances, we can recognize what kind of transgression we have committed. We find the key for this in the world of our thoughts and feelings.

If we do not know about reincarnation and the law of sowing and reaping, we are unable to interpret the vicissitudes of our life and draw false conclusions. We then remain on the surface of what happens; we compare, make value-judgments and, not seldom, we condemn. We see the one who used and exploited his neighbor, for whom things went well until his last breath, and the other one, whom we knew to be a friendly person, but who had to bear illness and suffering. Then perhaps we ask the question, "Is God a just God?"— Out of ignorance, many accuse God because He seems to mete out unjustly and arbitrarily, making people either poor or rich, sick or healthy and happy.

Let us return again to the statement of "reincarnation." If we were to take a closer look at it, we could gradually understand why different situations and occurrences come up in the life of each person. The knowledge about reincarnation helps us to recognize the just balance that is founded in the law of sowing and reaping. Through reincarnation, that is, by returning anew into the flesh, we first become aware of the meaning of life and that the inputs of one person come into effect today, and those of another, not until tomorrow.

Whoever recognizes reincarnation as the result of the law of balancing things out, "What a person sows, he will reap," also recognizes in this the justice of God, who neither favors nor disfavors any of His children. In His law, God has neither misery nor illness nor need. God's law of ever-giving love is for us: "Love God with all your heart, with all your soul and with all your might, and your neighbor as yourself."

Thus, if God has neither misery nor illness nor need in His law of love, He cannot mete out any of these, for where should He take them from, if He does not possess them? Why should God, who is the unending love, inflict punishment on His children, since He gave them the free will for a free decision, for or against Him? As the result of this freedom of decision, each one himself bears what he sows.

Our sufferings, no matter in what guise they appear, were caused by us through the sum of our negative actions. Within the principle of sending and receiving, we are in a constant exchange, in constant communication with our inputs, which are in the memory bank of our conscious mind and subconscious, of our soul, as well as of both cosmoses, the material cosmos and the cosmos of the purification planes. If a part of these inputs becomes active and pushes them to take effect, we will have to suffer them as human beings. If our soul is in the soul realms, then these active inputs could lead us to incarnation, providing that as human beings we want to clear up our sinfulness.

The person who studies the law of reincarnation knows that every cause has its effect and that every cause has to be expiated sooner or later, in this or in another life or in the spheres of purification—unless we recognize it in good time and clear it up.

The day speaks to us.
It shows us parts of our inputs
that we can clear up.
Desires in the will of the ego are reversed

he law of correspondence, which may produce a projection, helps us recognize our
causes bit by bit and in good time, and, with the
Redeemer-power of the Christ of God, to repent
of them, to clear them up and no longer commit this sinfulness. This is the Christian way. It is
plain and simple.

Christ shows us the direct path into freedom,
into happiness, into health and into peace, thus
guiding us into being near to God. This path
is: Recognize your sins; repent of them with all
your heart; clear them up with the help of Christ
who dwells in you; ask for forgiveness; forgive
also your neighbor who has sinned against you;
make amends as far as it is still possible and do
not commit this sin again. This is the very central

teaching of Jesus, the Christ, in His Sermon on the Mount.

If we follow this simple teaching, many things will change, little by little. Our behavior changes; our thoughts no longer circle around our own concerns; we become more selfless. Vitality and joy in life increase; it becomes easier and easier for us to discard the still existing base human aspects. We feel closer to God and to Christ; we are filled with gratitude and joy; our consciousness expands. In this way, we grow toward the fulfillment of the high commandment of love, until, like the pure beings of heaven, we can say, "God, my Father, I love You with all my heart, with all my strength, which You, Eternal One, have placed in me. My soul is filled with Your light. My brother, my sister, in the earthly garment are close to me; they are a part of me. Father, we thank You for Your kindness."

This is the way into the Father's house.

What human beings thought up—philosophies, rites, cults, sacraments, dogmas, doctrines of the most varying kind, the so-called traditions, institutions with their high-ranking ministers and priests, excellencies and gurus—all these are detours and are not the teaching of Jesus of Nazareth, the path to God.

Every day, every hour, every minute, every second, even every instant, is a help for us on our way. The components of our days on Earth often give us many possibilities to recognize and clear up, that is, to pay off, aspects of our sins, that is, of our correspondences that became a part of the world of our programs.

Whenever we get upset, when our face turns red, when we strike back outraged with words or gestures, or when we insult our fellow people in thoughts, when we disparage them, hate them, envy them this or that, the day is speaking to us. It shows us parts of our inputs. Threads of our web vibrate and show us, who have spun ourselves in like a spider, that here lies a sinful input.

If we live in the day, that is, if we are concentrated and focused on what we are presently supposed to be doing or taking care of, we will often catch ourselves during the day, when we become unsure of ourselves, when we fail in doing this or that, when, for example, something falls on our foot, when we stumble over a stone or a chair, or over the foot of our neighbor. If we are alert, then we perceive that the day is speaking to us and, because of what happened, wants to admonish us, to examine our feelings and thoughts and find out what lies behind them. In this way, we find the root of our sins and can clear them up according to the Christian commandments. Therefore, we need no ecclesiastical authorities, no sacraments, no confession and the like; we simply need the fulfillment of the highest commandment of love for God and neighbor.

If we follow the path of clearing up our sins the Christian way, then Christ in us transforms into light and power the sins we have repented of and cleared up. They are then erased from our soul and from the cosmoses of the Fall. These negative programs will also dissolve in our conscious mind and subconscious, because we then fulfill the commandments of God step by step. Whatever wrongdoing is cleared up and no longer taken up by us and no longer done, can also no longer come back to us. But whatever wrongdoing is and remains in us can, today or tomorrow or when we are disincarnate, that is, when we are in the soul realms, come toward us or befall our body in future incarnations.

Our situation would be hopeless if we did not have the Christ of God, our Redeemer. Whoever thinks that he can liberate himself with his own strength—which, in the last analysis, means to conquer his sin with sin—will have to recognize sooner or later that this is not the way to do it. For our personal life on a small scale, as well as for the doings of the world on a large scale, the following holds: Without the Christ of God, nothing is accomplished.

Once we are the masters of our own senses and thoughts, it will become still in us and God reveals Himself in the stillness. As long as our senses and thoughts have power over us, we are restless and driven, turned away from God and inclined toward sin. Then our sin manifests itself.

Whatever was sown and not remedied in good time, that is, not taken out of the acre of our soul, we will reap sooner or later. Thus, sooner or later, what we have once sown will show its effects on our body or in our immediate surroundings. For one person, this means that part of his inputs will become active in this life; for another, parts of his causes will gather like thunderclouds that will rain down on him in another incarnation. Or the discarnate soul will bear the burden of its guilt in the form of pain and suffering in the purification planes, on those planets where its inputs, its negative energies, are stored as pictures.

Many people have fallen victim to a false teaching that says: You may wish for anything you want. You need only to send out the same thoughts over and over again and what you wish for will be fulfilled. But Jesus taught us, "Seek first the Kingdom of God and His righteousness and all else will be given to you." This means that we should first open up our divine heritage, the Kingdom of God, in ourselves. We need to let the power of Christ become manifest in our thinking and acting, and then God will give us what we need—not what we want.

The energy of our thoughts, of our wanting and desires, that is, of our inputs, presses toward realization. What we desire and want over and over again, and thus input, will be fulfilled in one form or another. However, if we have not opened up the inner kingdom with the key, Christ, if we have not brought to light the treasure of our inner being, who will it be then, who fulfills the actions of our will? Certainly not Christ, but the one who rules this world. And that one demands repayment to the last penny, for the energy he has invested in order to fulfill our desires for us. The adversary knows neither grace nor forgiveness. For him, what is valid is, "An eye for an eye and a tooth for a tooth," down to the last penny.

Therefore, it can lead to grave consequences for us when we delude ourselves and live in a fantasy world of desires which says, "I want money and possessions. I want a princely home. I want 'slaves' who work for me. I want. I want power, wealth and prestige. I want, I want …"

Perhaps we think these are thought games that bring no one harm if they are not realized. But the wanting of a person can become a trap for him. Let us consider the following:

Whatever we want, we have not worked for, because we have not acquired the kingdom of the inner being, having not opened it through a life according to the laws of God. As a result, one day, the will of our ego will reverse itself; our wanting will turn against us. And why?

A thought that is within the law, within the will of God, already bears its fulfillment in itself. On the Earth, too, it will be fulfilled; it is only a question of time.

But if our will is not the divine "let there be," because it contains the wanting to take and not to give, we are not in the stream, in the law of God. And then, according to the law of sowing and reaping, it is, "As you have taken, so will it be taken from you."

Thus, our egoistic inputs will be fulfilled in their own way, in the law of sowing and reaping. Therefore, in the end, we will have neither money nor goods, but will live in poverty. Instead of a princely house, we may own a mud hut. Instead of ordering around servants and "slaves," we will have to do slave work ourselves somewhere. Instead of enjoying power, wealth and prestige, we will be stripped of power, be worthless people to the world, without money or prestige, who may have to work hard for their bread or even have to beg for it.

Perhaps the prince of this world will at first fulfill the will of our ego, because through the constant repetition of the input, "I want, I want," we set free forces that fulfill what we want. But this is then a loan from the negative forces and no gift from God. What we have will not only be taken from us, but we will have to suffer from the fact that we have purloined energies instead of generating energies by opening up the inner kingdom.

Nothing happens by chance.
Our correspondences mark us.
Everyone is themselves responsible for their
own inputs

othing, but nothing, happens by chance. Everything that constitutes our life, down to the finest nuances of our body posture and the most inconspicuous situations of our days, is pre-determined by us. For every single one of our inputs, we, the individual, are responsible. The law of sowing and reaping calls us to account.

Let's think about the words of Jesus who spoke in the following sense, "Even the hairs on your head are counted." "Counted" means that even though one hair is only the tiniest detail of a person, it is, nevertheless, recorded.

Likewise, there are no chance occurrences in the nature kingdoms. From the creation laws of nature, everything is cosmic storing and cosmic guidance. The life forms in nature cannot burden themselves. There is no wrongdoing in them. According to the share of the individual in the collective guilt of humankind toward nature, each one of us will be charged for what we do to nature by changing the laws of creation.

For many centuries, the human being has posed as the lord, the creator, of nature, so to speak, thinking he can do better than God. Instead of respecting, cherishing and loving the ruling hand of God, he took and takes the Creator's scepter into his own hands and exploits nature. The results are causes under which all of humankind is already suffering.

Each one of us is himself responsible for his inputs. The wife, the husband, the mother, the mother-in-law, the father-in-law, the child, the colleague, the boss cannot be held responsible for our inputs. Just as we call into the canyon, that is how it echos back. Our seed is the call into the canyon, and our harvest is the echo that comes back.

The usual objection is, "But if my wife, my husband, my father-in-law, my colleague has tried my patience and provoked me, am I supposed to be responsible for my anger?"

Yet we should ask ourselves, "Why was the threshold of my anger so low that my neighbor was able to provoke me?" It is because in our soul and in our conscious mind and subconscious, we have correspondences that are similar to those of our fellow person who was or still is an annoyance to us. The moment of vexation is a hint from the energy of our day that knocks at our conscience and says, "Look at yourself, why you are so upset? Which of your feelings, thoughts, words or actions called up this strong emotion?"

If we watch, for example, our body posture during the moments of our irritation, or where we look to, what we reach for, where we go, what we neglect, or who in our surroundings annoys us at the moment, then we experience a part of our correspondences, our programs, which control us and shape our body, marking it.

If at the moment of our strongest irritation we had a mirror at hand, this would be very helpful, "Mirror, mirror on the wall, my correspondences, you show them invariably."

Some wrinkles become deeper, we frown, our face turns gray, pale or red. Whole sections of our face change; our lips are pressed together; the corners of our mouth turn down; our expression becomes somber; our eyes are spitting envy, revenge, rejection, rage.

Let's try it—it is worth our while for the sake of self-recognition. Perhaps then it will be easier for us to feel remorse and to clear things up.

Our agitations come from the individual programs, from our correspondences. We react, according to the reason for our agitation, whether fear or rage.

If we are constantly under tension, that is, if our thoughts are in a constant state of alarm from morning to late at night, we will become either negligent or indifferent, or we react with quarreling and violence.

The results of this constant stress through our correspondences mark us more and more. We become lazy and passive or aggressive, for example, depending on what our correspondences signal to us.

The external letting-oneself-go is often a sign of great external or internal unrest. Then, our hair is no longer orderly; our shoes are scruffy; our gait is heavy; our face is furrowed; our whole appearance is either sluggish or extremely tense and ready to attack. Then we neglect our home, which we clean up only to the point of being barely presentable. Our clothing hardly means anything to us anymore. We become indifferent to color and form, not to mention our body, which may begin to increase in weight and volume—by taking in too much food and hard drinks. Old behavior patterns, which we believed to have overcome, reappear.

Many changes! And why? Because some of our correspondences, our causes, are active. At some point in time, they will break in over us as effects, if we do not use the moments and situations that made us angry or stressful to clear things up in order to free ourselves from these causes with the help of our Redeemer, Christ.

All of infinity is life and evolution.
The forms of the nature kingdoms are
degrees of consciousness in God's stream
of creation

The innermost being in each one of us is the bearer of the Kingdom of God and the heir to infinity; it is the law, God. Our physical body, however, belongs to the Earth, to the physical laws of nature. It is the bearer of, and heir to, our sinfulness.

Thus, everything is law, either the law of the Eternal, of eternity, or the law of sinfulness, which has its effects on the Earth and in the purification planes. The law of correspondence, the sinfulness, cannot last, because God is not sin, but the pure One who created all things pure.

Everything that is egotistical, the sinfulness, will become pure again, through the absolute, irrevocable law of love, but only with our active cooperation, since each one of us is a bearer of free will.

At some point in time—even if it is after many sojourns on Earth—our innermost being awakens, which then wants to strive unerringly and directly toward its eternal homeland. Then, soul and person, too, are willing to fulfill the divine heritage, the Kingdom of God in us.

Everything pure, everything that is in God, is the law of God, the love. The nature kingdoms in the eternal Being are the active laws of evolution of the Creator, the Spirit of God. The kingdom of nature unfolds in the most diverse levels of development. Every level of development is a state of evolution in the kingdoms of the minerals, plants and tiniest animals. Depending on their species and state of development, they are all grouped into collectives, which radiate their form and color of consciousness. Every degree of consciousness, that is, every collective consciousness, is a facet of evolution out of the whole, the life, God. The totality, God, is always in the smallest as well as in the large, indivisibly. Every form of life, according to its state of consciousness, is a facet of the revelation of God.

All levels of consciousness are respirated by the mighty Creator-Spirit, who leads them to perfection, that is, to the unfoldment of the totality. In all the facets of evolution of the most varied levels of development, the Creator-Spirit takes on form and shape according to the state of consciousness. They are the expression of His love. And yet, in each facet, He is the totality, indivisible.

It is the same in the kingdoms of the animals, which have reached the evolutionary state of part spirit-bodies, which are also called part-souls. Here, too, there are the most varied species of animals, which manifest themselves in their corresponding colors and forms, according to the development of the part spirit-body. Evolution leads from simple forms with only one segment, one aspect, to the developed part spirit-body, which then passes into the evolutionary state of the nature being. In these different degrees of consciousness of the animals, which radiate color and form according to the development of their part spirit-body, God is, in turn, the revelation of the form. Yet He is and remains always the whole in every segment of evolution. Whether we contemplate the stars or the components of matter, God is always in all things, the whole, indivisible.

In all of infinity there is nothing rigid, or even dead. Everything is filled with life, with the Spirit. Everything is energy, even if we speak of "dead matter." If matter breaks down into its component parts, what changes is only its radiation, its vibration, which corresponds to its momentary substance.

In the Spirit of God there is constant evolution. The primordial power, God, respirates infinity in a predetermined rhythm. The life forms of primordial substance of the nature kingdoms in the eternal Being, into which God breathes increased energy at cyclic intervals, evolve into the next higher forms of life. In this evolutionary course of rhythmic and cyclical respiration of the spiritual nature kingdoms, the pure beings, called spirit beings, emerged.

The term "spirit being" means that all pure beings came and come forth from the evolutionary law, the primordial stream, God, the love and wisdom. The spiritual body, the spirit being, is spirit that took on form; we could also say, the law of God that took on form. Every spirit being is the image of the eternal Father, who gave Himself the form out of His eternal primordial stream, also called Creator-stream, out of His eternal omnipresent law of love and wisdom. The spiritual body, which builds up from the evolutionary law, the stream of creation of the spiritual mineral, plant and animal kingdoms, is complete only once it has gone through all the levels of spiritual evolution, including the sonship and daughtership of God.

Once the spiritual body is complete, that is, once the spirit being is the son or daughter of God, then this spiritual body, which is spiritual substance that took on form, that is, compressed light-force, has gone through all the evolutionary levels, so that the spirit being is the law of love of God. The law of love is the Father-Mother-Law, because God, the stream of creation, consists of the two poles, Father and Mother, male and female. Spiritually speaking, God is giving as well as receiving.

The spiritual suns and planets, which are pure primordial substance that took on form, also are a part of the eternal law, God. The energetic substances of the suns and planets of primordial substance are a lawful component of the spiritual body of every completed being. Because of this, every completed divine-spiritual body bears the heritage of infinity. Since every spiritual body is a bearer of the spiritual heritage, thus combining in itself the essence of all forces, absolute freedom is given to every being. Through this cosmic-primordial heritage, based on the structure of the spiritual-divine body, which is the law of eternity and thus a completed spiritual-divine form of primordial substance, a spirit being can move on all the pathways of the stars. All the planets of the pure Being have been opened up in the spiritual body. Since God is omnipresent and the pure being is divine through the cosmic-primordial heritage, it has full access to all the cosmoses, including those of the purification planes and of matter.

The Fall-beings created their own personal heritage with their world of programs. The burdens of the individual determine his future incarnations

In the Fall-event, pure spirit beings turned away from God not only in order to not be divine, but to become God themselves. In this way, these divine light-forms separated from God and created their first world of programs for wanting to be like God. Through this, the spiritual-divine body became shadowed and, in countless cosmic sequences, increasingly densified, out of which the human body crystallized.

In the word "Fall" lies the word "fallen." Through the Fall of some spirit beings, that is, by their turning away from God, parts of divine planets of primordial substance also separated and went with the spirit beings into the depths. In the course of the Fall-event, they served and still serve as places of residence for the Fall-beings. All parts of the planets of primordial substance took on the corresponding form and density according to the condensation of the spirit beings. The once pure beings shadowed their divine heritage with their world of programs, which built on the desire to be like God, and created more and more their personal heritage-law that corresponded to their Fall-thoughts.

For understanding: A fine-material body, the soul, dwells within the human being, the physical shell. The soul garments, which are the radiation of the shadowed soul, envelop our spiritual body, our eternal being. They also form the aura of the person.

Our divine body consists of the essence of infinity and is thus the bearer of the eternal law, God, through which we are sons and daughters of God—also as human beings. All human beings bear within the cosmic-primordial heritage of the eternal Being, the spiritual-divine body, which they have overshadowed and surrounded with their sinfulness, with their heritage of burdens.

Our present physical body was formed from the genetic make-up of our ancestors and parents, some of whom we were ourselves. Those who know about reincarnation come to the logical conclusion that their soul came as a human being into the earthly life again and again in past incarnations and thus, via this genetic chain, contributed to covering up their divine heritage.

What we bear today that is far from God, that is sinful, is our yesterday. In one or several of our lives on Earth, we have input what we are today and what we may have to suffer under today. That is our sinful heritage, the turning-away from God and from our divine heritage. This heritage of burdens marks our physical body and our soul.

If we do not expiate this as a soul in the beyond, then our soul brings its sinfulness with it again, into a new life on Earth. Since like always attracts like, we come over and over again to those people whom we have sinned against or into whom we have projected a part of our sins. We are bound to them, so that we may clear up with each other what drew us together. We meet each other again in the roles of father, mother, child, relatives, friends, work colleagues, superiors and the like. Yesterday, I had the role of the father; today, I am a child in the same family. Yesterday, I was the boss; today, I am in the role of an employee of the boss of this company. Yesterday, I was the mother; today, I am part of this family as a relative. We also choose the places for our earthly life according to our active sinful heritage, our world of programs.

God created heaven and Earth.
The spiritual events behind the "Big Bang"

God gave His children—the Fall-beings who wanted to be like God and who created their own personal imprinting laws, their sinful heritage—dwelling places, which are like return stations, parts of pure spiritual planets which, as already mentioned, condensed little by little with the imprinting of the Fall-beings. All people and souls, as well as all condensed planets, bear the unburdened and incorruptible eternal core of the being of life, God. Since God is thus present in all things, He will also lead all things back into the eternal Being.

It is written in the following sense: God created heaven and Earth and made the human being in His image. This means that God loves all His children, including those who turned away from Him. This is why He gave them parts of spiritual celestial bodies to take with them. In the course of countless cycles—we would say in, for us, unimaginably long periods of time—these formed the planets of the purification planes, where the souls of deceased human beings live and the planets of the material cosmos like the Earth, on which the people live.

Science speaks of the so-called "Big Bang" that triggered the formation of matter. In a certain way, the big bang theory is in accordance with the spiritual principles that triggered the separation of sin, that is, density, from the pure all-pervading Being. This unimaginable process of separation brought about frothing turbulences, which we human beings describe as the Big Bang.

The purification planes, which are of a finer substance, and matter, which is dense material, form the Fall-realms. Matter as well as the purification planes are levels which souls and people have to pass through in order to become again and be what they are at the core of their soul, in the very basis of their soul: pure beings from God and in God.

God is indivisible—as already explained. He is the power, the spirit, the life—also outside of the heavens, in all the Fall-realms and in all their forms, forces and elements. There is only one life; it is the Eternal and eternity, indivisible in all things. Since God is the indivisible, eternal life and without Him nothing can exist, God is also the life in the planets outside the divine kingdoms in all life forms of nature, in souls and in human beings.

God I s —The spirit beings are divine.
God is the expression of spiritual forms.
He is i n the material forms,
but is not the material form itself

For the sake of clarification may the difference between "God is" and "God is in …" be explained once more.

In the Kingdom of God, in the eternal heavens, it is: God is the Kingdom of God. God is the revelation and expression of all the facets of creation of the purely spiritual planets and worlds. God is the expression and revelation of the pure spirit beings.

Out of His eternal omnipresent stream, God created and creates forms of creation, that is, forms of evolution. He is every form of evolution of the pure nature kingdoms.

Out of His infinitely eternal, omnipresent stream, the eternal law, God gave Himself form. The expression of the stream I AM is the Eternal, and the Eternal is the complete divine form, the pure, fine-material primordial substance: the eternal Father, the highest Intelligence of the Being, the form that bears the eternal consciousness of the infinitely eternal Spirit: I was and Am eternally.

The form of God-Father is the consciousness of light before creation, the light of the creation-thought, the light of creation itself, the expression of infinite eternity, the Eternal, the I Am. His children are His creation-thoughts. As children of light, they are heirs to creation that were and are active participants in the creation of the Being.

The primordial stream, the Spirit, is also called the Father-Mother-Stream, because He, the eternal Father, gave Himself form from it and created and creates from it His children, the spirit beings. God calls all forms "divine," which came and come forth from the primordial stream, the Father-Mother-Stream.

In the eternal pure Being, God is not "in the form." He *is* Himself the complete divine form, the Father, and is Himself the expression of the complete forms of the spirit beings. He is Creator and expression of all evolutionary facets, which He leads to completion. Each completed form, each spirit being, is the divine law itself and is heir to the pure Being. The completed pure forms, the divine beings, are not omnipresent, but are all-conscious. They are subject to no limitations because they are heirs to all pure forces, heirs to the eternal law of love, and, at the same time, are the law of love itself.

Therefore, the beings in God, the spirit beings, are not omnipresent, but are absolutely free, without limitation in their perception and mobility. Their home is the infinity because they are the inhabitants and heirs to infinity. Every ray of light of the Being is their divine heritage; it serves them. Solely the primordial stream, the flowing law, God, the love, is omnipresent, indivisible in all things.

The Fall-realms, including matter, are not the expression of God and are not the divine that has taken on form; but God, the indivisible, the primordial stream, the all-ruling law of love, is *in* the stars, *in* the nature kingdoms, *in* the souls and *in* human beings.

Thus, in the Fall-realms to which matter belongs, God is not the form; instead, He is *in* the forms. God is *in* the four elements of matter, in every particle, in every atom, in every molecule. However, He is not matter itself.

The material stars and the stars of the purification planes are not spirit that has taken on form; instead, God is *in* the material stars and *in* the stars of the purification planes. God is in every component of the physical body, in every cell. God is not the component of the body, not the cell. God is not the form of the physical body; instead, He is *in* the form. God is not the form of the minerals, plants and animals either. God is *in* the form of the minerals, plants and animals.

Therefore, God is in all the condensed forms, but is not the condensed form itself. This developed through the imprintings of the Fall, through the sinful heritage of every human being. Through the sinful behavior of a human being, his soul shapes the planets of the purification planes, which absorb these inputs as vibrations, and also the outer forms of the nature kingdoms.

Our physical body is merely a pale reflection of our divine, pure form, which is the image of God-Father and the revelation of God.

Thus, the human being is not the expression of God, but the expression of his soul. Whatever is active in the soul shows its effects in and on the body. This is the sinful heritage of every person, which imprints his physical genetic make-up, his genes. From this, the character of every single individual is formed, his inclinations, his passions, his concepts, his desires, his feelings, his thoughts, words and actions.

The physical body is an expression of the world of programs of soul and person.

The perfection of the pure body is the expression of God. The divine heritage marks the spiritual body just as the expression of sin marks the physical body. Sin is turning away from God and shadowing the soul, covering up the light. The human being is called to let his soul again become the image of God, of the eternal Father, by repenting of the sinfulness he recognizes each day, by clearing it up and no longer committing it. Thus, the human being is on Earth to raise his soul again to the image of God, the eternal Father.

Humankind does not descend from the apes. The becoming of human beings. Matter is the human will that took on form

There are many opinions and theories in this world about the emergence of humankind. Some say that the human body developed via the plant and animal kingdoms, that in its last phase of development it descended from the apes. Only few mention the Fall-thought, the beings of light who wanted to be like God, and the condensation which, in the end, led to the human body.

Evolution—which, in the spirit, is rhythms and cycles, that is, the leaps from mineral to plant, from plant to animal, from animal via nature beings to a perfect life form like that of the spirit beings—exists only in the pure Being.

In the kingdom of heaven, this spiritual evolution takes place from one spiritual atom—comparable to a human cell—via the spiritual kingdoms of the minerals, plants and animals, all the way to the spiritual forms of the nature beings, from which the perfect spiritual body gradually emerges. Since the spiritual body is built up via all the forces of God, the perfect spirit being is the All-heir, the Absolute Law. Because of this, it is in communication with all pure cosmic forces since it came forth from these forces, that is, it became a spiritual-divine form in a lawful process.

The perfect being from God is in every human being—it is, however, burdened by sin, and for this reason is called soul. Therefore, our physical body can never have descended from the apes, even if similarities come up here and there. These similarities developed through the programming of the Fall-beings, and later through human beings, but never through the material nature kingdoms.

The spirit beings who wanted to be like God and thus became Fall-beings—who created their own personal condensation thoughts as their personal heritage, who wanted to be lords and rulers with their own personal kingdoms and subjects—first created their personal envelopment of burdens, that is, they enveloped themselves with the negative energies of their own desires, feelings and thoughts.

The forces that were energetically transformed down streamed from the burdened spiritual particles of the spiritual bodies of the Fall-beings. They formed gas-like shells, as it were, which settled around the Fall-being like an aura. The continued violations against the divine law meant a continuous burdening, through which these shells became ever denser over unimaginably long courses of time.

Thus, the first Fall-beings enveloped themselves with their sinful feelings and thoughts, their Fall-feelings and Fall-thoughts. As a result of this continuous violation against their divine heritage, the density that we call "human being" emerged very gradually. Just as these spirit beings enveloped and condensed with their radiation, they also enveloped and condensed the spiritual parts of the planets that served as their dwelling places.

The spiritual body of the Fall-beings was enveloped in different ways during the course of their descent into becoming a human being. The gaslike mantle, the shell, of the one was denser, of the other lighter, according to how great or small the shadowing of the individual Fall-being was. The principle was then, and is still today, valid for every person: According to how the Fall-being felt, thought and acted, it shadowed and condensed itself. According to how a person feels, thinks, speaks and acts, he shapes himself.

As it was at the time of the Fall, so it is still today for us people: Some thought and think, acted and act more thoughtfully, striving to do right; others, however, acted and act ever more against the divine law. Accordingly, the Fall-being enveloped itself, and accordingly the person shapes his character and his physical body.

According to the principle "like attracts like," the same and similarly condensed beings attracted each other. According to their degree of condensation, which corresponded to their world of desires, they influenced their dwelling planets, as already explained. These then also enveloped themselves with the same or like vibrations as their inhabitants. The same principle applies to the highest degree of condensation, which is the human being: Like attracts like. According to their sinfulness, the inhabitants have a negative influence on their dwelling planet, the Earth.

In the pure Being, everything is law, but also in the spheres that were transformed down, everything is "law." In the Fall-realms and on matter, life took and takes place exactly like it is in the pure Being—only reversed. The divine law is the divine heritage of every spirit being. The sinfulness of every individual person is his own personal law, his imprinting and character. The material principles and forms of the nature kingdoms, too, are reversals of the divine law of creation, of the natural laws of the pure Being.

What shaped the Fall-beings, the programs of their wanting and desires, was also their emitting potential. In the same way, the individual imprinting of every person, which consists of countless programs, is, in turn, his emitting potential, with which he works. While the pure beings fulfill the will of God, the Fall-beings refused to do this. They programmed and imprinted themselves with their self-will; and according to this, they acted.

It is the same with people. The self-will of a person is his imprinting. With this, he acts in his environment and affects others.

In, for human beings, unimaginably long processes since the beginning of the Fall, which take place in rhythms and cycles, the hardest density, matter, emerged. Through the sinful behavior of every single human being, matter has become the human will, which took on form. While the shells of the soul became ever denser, the structure of the physical body crystallized from this, corresponding in its entire construction to the currents and processes of the material cosmos.

As suns can give birth to planets through the influence of energetic forces in the material cosmic process, so does the woman, through the procreation of the man, give birth to a body for the soul that comes from finer-material spheres to incarnate on Earth. In this way, the possibility for a cycle of coming and going to the Earth is created for a soul—the so-called wheel of reincarnation. In every vivified body there is a soul that slips into it at birth and that slips out of the material body at death.

The one who transforms the forces of procreation and preservation into sensual lust sins against God's force of creation. The one who instills his own programs into others shows with this an energy deficit, or weakness

In the very basis of every soul is the incorruptible core of being, which contains the creation force of the Creator. All in all, this is the divine inheritance of every pure being. Since God is in the soul of the human being, the human being can be called a pale reflection of the divine.

God, the Creator, constantly breathes in and out. He, the Creator-force, is also the energy of evolution in the divine nature kingdoms, in the four creation-forces of God: Order, Will, Wisdom and Earnestness. The creation-force of God in every human being is the force of procreation and preservation, the Father-Mother-Principle.

The procreation and birth of a child are totally normal processes. They are a pale reflection of the creation force of God. But the one who transforms the force of procreation and preservation into sensual lust sins against the law of nature, against the Father-Mother-Principle.

With the sensual lusts, we influence our five senses. With the kind of sensual lusts that are programs, we stimulate our five senses and, via our five senses, our whole behavior. The result is our feeling, thinking, speaking and acting. Our behavior, which corresponds to our programmed senses, then, in turn, has its effect on our sensual desires. In this way, the world of our programs, which is always and again we ourselves, strengthens and condenses. This world of our programs is our creative tool.

If we equate our sensual desires with sexuality, which then merely serves to gratify our lusts and to relax our nervous system, then it becomes compulsive. In such dissipation we waste unimaginable amounts of drawing and creating energy. This is a sin against the Creator-force and leads to an energy deficit through which we become lazy, negligent or deviant. "Deviant" in this context refers to the compulsive programs of the base, all-too-human drives. This deviance, in turn, shapes our character and our physical body.

Our sinful heritage makes us blind and often causes us to interpret the impulses from our soul in a wrong way. Then we go looking in the wrong direction.

The divine heritage that is in the innermost part of the soul of every person is the life in the light, in the fullness of colors, forms, fragrances and sounds, in peace, in a state of being fulfilled, which could be described as the everlasting presence of God. If the longing for peace vibrates upward from the basis of our soul into our person, into our world of programs, then the person seeks to satisfy this longing. And then, for example, the relaxation that follows the physical act reflects to him the fulfillment of this longing.

But since this "peace" is illusory and the relaxation is only of short duration, the person and the senses keep looking. Further thoughts, desires and thus, programs are formed—seeking programs which, not seldom, become addictive programs. Perhaps the person resorts to pleasures in order to fill the emptiness, for example, with good and plentiful meals. He fills his stomach, and yet remains empty of fulfillment. He takes, perhaps ever more, alcoholic drinks, and yet the spirit of the wine does not bring with it spirituality, the expansion of consciousness that is based on a life according to the commandments of God.

The palette of off-shoots, of secondary programs, of programs of the all-too-human, is a colorful mixture. Part of this is the addiction to diversions—like, for example, watching TV every evening, the need for strong stimulants like those that come from hard music, the magic of disco lights, wild parties and much more.

Whether it is gluttony or the excessive consumption of alcoholic drinks, whether the addiction for enhancement or passions of other kinds, including the behavior of lust, the abnormality, we imprint our soul and our physical genetic make-up. They are immensely active programs that seek out people of like mind in order to influence and control them. Those who allow this to happen, that is, who let themselves be controlled, are bound to their programmer, who can now continue to influence them, since like always attracts like.

The negative equivalents are designed in their program specifications to determine and control others. Why is this so?

God, the eternal source of energy of the pure Being, gives inexhaustibly. The positive exchange, giving and receiving, the positive communication, links us with the eternal stream, the highest source of energy, God.

The communication on the human level, in all-too-humanness, in sinfulness, in the world of our human programs, is an exchange of human energy. God is always there for us with His power, if we turn to Him in order to draw closer to Him. But He does not support our negativity, our sins. Therefore, our sinful programs depend on the supply of human energy, negative energy.

In the exchange of correspondences—for example, applauding one's neighbor in order to receive his energy, his good will—the energy is soon exhausted. A lack of energy is the result. Since God does not give His energy for this, consciously or unconsciously, the search for more energy begins, and finally, the craving for it. By way of projection, the person then endeavors to dominate and influence others, that is, to program them and gain them as dependents, as sources of energy.

Someone who dominates others and imposes his will on them does not do this out of strength—even though it may seem this way—but from a lack of energy, from a weakness. In order to reach his goal, he cleverly uses the weaknesses of his neighbor and does not respect the latter's free will. This is why the victim of his manipulation can evade this influence only by recognizing his own weaknesses and overcoming them with the help of the Christ of God.

Very briefly, here is another variant in the broad range of the law of correspondence and of projection:

For the sake of the alleged strengths and merits of their neighbor, a category of people enters into a dependency; we could call them "imitators." In the absence of any strength and merits of their own, they lean on one or more of their fellow people, in order to live in their reflection, as it were, to have a share in their life, and to bask in their would-be radiance.

As imitators, we take on the peculiarities of the other's behavior, of his manner of speech, his way of living, in order to deck ourselves out with borrowed plumes, to exalt ourselves, and to be like our role model, whom we attribute with certain values that we lack.

The correspondences and human programs of our neighbor that we adopt are the human ballast that we have to overcome, to clear up or to expiate its consequences. When we become imitators, we drift away from ourselves and perceive the tasks and possibilities of our life on Earth not at all or only partly. We are then bound to the person whose programs we have copied. The other person is bound to us to the extent that he gained some advantage from this, and be it, for example, by accepting the "admiration-energy."

The fans of "idols" also belong to this category, whether in the areas of music, film, sports, politics or science. Prominent and popular figures and others often serve as "role-models" who attract "imitators" as described above.

Many, many people are bound, caught in their own web and in the web of others. Only once we recognize our dependency, our binding, can the Christ of God, our Redeemer, help us to become free step by step on the path of purification.

In the book, "The Inner Path, Level of Earnestness" we read the following: The ego of a person can exert influence on his fellow people only until they no longer pay tribute to their own base ego and raise their consciousness more and more to God. The quickest way for the baseness to leave a person is when he entrusts himself to God in every situation.

With our sinful inheritance we have covered our divine heritage, so that we are no longer aware of who we truly are. We have not lost the divine in us, although this seems to be the case, because it is covered through our sinfulness. For the person who considers his sham world to be reality, his sinful inheritance is the truth that he views as the highest. This is what we then call "our life," our "self-esteem" that we defend with all means available to us, even to the point of acts of war, where one nation rises against another.

Therefore, our life is our world of programs, either a potential for work or a battle axe. Thus, our personal world of programs controls us, inducing us to think, say or do this or that.

*A person who is externally programmed
hardly lives his own life anymore;
he lacks feelings and is controlled.
A world-encompassing web of karma and
a worldwide genetic chain*

Every person is surrounded by his own world of programs; it is his aura; it is he himself. Everything is energy, and thus, vibration. The one body vibrates at a lower rate, the other higher, depending on the person's world of programs.

If we human beings speak about spirit and matter, we often describe matter as density. But density is not simply dense; it depends on the vibration frequency of the body. The physical body is an expression of its vibration frequency and of its environment, which together shape the form.

As the Fall began, the Fall-beings lived in accordance with their degree of condensation on the dwelling planet that corresponded to their state of consciousness, to their vibration frequency. Once the coarse-material substance, the human body, crystallized into being, life on Earth began for humankind. The Earth is inhabited by people of all degrees of consciousness, that is, those with a higher or lower consciousness, sinners and purified ones, idlers and workers, criminals and righteous ones.

A person who does not orient himself to the commandments of God, and thus, does not walk the path back to his origin that is divine, weakens himself through his own sins. Depending on his sinfulness, the one tries to influence the other, because sin always urges us to be the greatest. Our sins, which are our correspondences, want to know themselves confirmed in others, so as to draw energy from this. For this reason, we are always trying to program our neighbors, that is, to influence them, to infect them, by instilling our own concepts in them. A person who allows his neighbor to program him by insinuation, that is, who allows one of his fellow people to implant his abnormality into him, can, as already mentioned, become alienated from his nature. He is partly no longer himself, but the other.

Through this influence, through manipulation, it is possible that a person who has become programmed from without can hardly live his own life anymore, that he can no longer perceive the impulses of the day that show him his sinfulness that needs to be cleared up. This is because these external programs overlie the world of his own life, the world of his programs, and take effect again and again, constantly dominating him. In time, such a person becomes emotionally impoverished.

Because of these implanted external programs that are active and in communication with their programmer, the person thus programmed can always be influenced and directed by him without realizing it. These active external programs then become a part of his life. They are the basis of his thinking and speaking. Often without noticing it, he builds further programs on these external programs, which may be similar to the programs for his life, but are never his life.

A person who dominates his neighbor, that is, who insinuates into the latter his own correspondences, has a willing instrument, namely, his neighbor, who does what his programmer wants as if under compulsion. He is dependent and controlled from without. He is robbed of a part of his free will to the point of enslavement. His programmer can make him dance and hop about on the strings of his weaknesses like a puppeteer with his marionette. In the end, it will be of little use to the one who is controlled from without to accuse his manipulator or to try to pay him back in the same, all-too-human coin. He will free himself from his clutches only when he recognizes his weaknesses, clears them up and develops divine values and strengths with the help of the Christ of God.

Through this negative influence, the one is bound to the other. If both, having equally vibrating programs, project their correspondences, their programs, their sinfulness, into other people, then a web of karma is formed that builds a chain of influences, as it were. Thus, the virus of projection can be transmitted to other people.

Every implanted external program marks the one who has taken it in. Through the principle of sending and receiving, he will resemble the one who has controlled him or still controls him. Based on the law of "like draws to like," both will then meet one another again and again, either in this world or as souls in the purification planes or in further incarnations. Their correspondences will either collide or complement each other. It all depends on what additional programs both have built up.

The result of all these processes is a world-spanning web of karma, into which many people and souls are interwoven, indeed, even knotted and matted into one another. Connected with this is also the worldwide chain of genes, because a person passes on his genes in many different ways; the exchange of genes through the sexual act is only one of many possibilities.

Our human programs are recorded in our brain, in our soul and in the stars, as well as in our genes. If we take over the program of another, this also is reflected in our genes. Based on its genetic make-up, which can also be pre-dispositions of burdens, a soul, which, for example, lived in Europe in a former incarnation, may now incarnate in Asia, because there parts of its burdened genes, which it transmitted, are now active in an Asian person.

No person can escape his own shadow. At some point everyone has to look at his sinfulness, the countless aspects of his world of programs, in order to clear it up.

Telepathic influencing of one's neighbor gives rise to the deed.
Results of binding via projections in specific examples

I t doesn't sound in any way dramatic when we hear that one person transmits a part of his world of thoughts to another by way of telepathic influence; both are now bound to each other. But what does such a process look like specifically, and what can be the consequences?

An example: A person who is seized by extreme jealousy furiously swears revenge against his rival, producing the corresponding thoughts. Whether or not these thoughts find an echo in the object of his jealousy, his thoughts swarm out, so to speak, and via telepathy reach, through the attraction of like types, one of his fellow people who has absolutely nothing to do with him or his jealousy, but who has in himself the same propensity toward taking revenge.

The latter may be hatching something similar in the same vein himself. He is devising plans of revenge, thinking about how to craftily clear the field of his rival, but always refrains from carrying out his plan. Either he is held back by thoughts of discovery, or he listens to the warning of his conscience. But when in a "weak moment," the emotionally laden thought buzzing around in the atmosphere from the heart of the first jealous person flies at him, he willingly accepts and takes in this "vagabond thought."

This means that the destructive rage, which is carried by the vagabond thought, "If only I could do as I want, I would do it," reinforces the waves of fury in the brooding person and his reservations disappear. He hesitates no longer, flatly shuts off his conscience and carries out what he has long since prepared in his thoughts. And so, we have not only an instigator and a perpetrator, we also have the "first" victim.

The perpetrator thinks that he was the one who made the decision to act. In reality, he took over the impulse to act from the thoughts of the instigator, to him unknown, who, filled with rage, entered the thought into the atmosphere, "I would do it."

Instigator and perpetrator are now bound to each other. The cosmic computer registers every quantum, for it is just. Each will be precisely allocated his part of the guilt, instigator as well as perpetrator. According to their share of guilt, both are involved and bound to one another. This means that, together, they must expiate what ties them to each other, including what resulted and still results from it.

Let us assume that because of his cleverness, the perpetrator remains undiscovered and is not punished by worldly laws. His guilt will be revealed to the other participant at the latest, when the latter has put aside his earthly garment. The waves of base human emotions will then surge high again, when this karma becomes active through the irradiation of the repository planets.

If one of the two now passes away—for example, the perpetrator—and feels as a soul that this common guilt between them is being activated by the stars, then it is possible that the soul of the deceased exerts an intense influence on the person to whom it is bound.

The radiation from the stars wants to stimulate both the soul and the person to clear up the common guilt with each other and also with their other victims. If neither person nor soul make use of this opportunity, then the following may happen: Through the radiation of the stars, the still hate-filled soul can—if the other guilty party is within the span of death—influence its accomplice so intensely, the human being, that the latter may die earlier than was meant for him in his life plan.

How does the soul exert influence on the accomplice who is still in an earthly garment? Through their common input in the repository planets, the soul makes injections. Either it intensifies an illness that is partly connected to their common karma, or it drives the person into extreme agitation so that, for example, a heart attack may occur, or it intensely influences his soul vibration so that he violates the laws of the state and perhaps passes on shortly thereafter as a result of great suffering and despair. Or the soul has such an intense effect on him that he causes an accident and thereby dies. Or, because his nervous system is shattered and he is utterly racked by aggressions and depressions, the person brings his life on Earth to an end.

The soul, which cannot forgive the other guilty party for his influence, wants to avenge itself in this way. The person, who is the target of these activities of the soul may not know what is happening until the hour of his death. He could recognize it if he were to pay attention to the hints from the energy of the day. If he were to recognize himself in his own causes, in his feelings of oppression, his thoughts, feelings and irritations, in his anxieties, his aggressions or in the reappearance of old programs, deemed long since overcome, then, by way of the path of purification, he would be able to largely avoid the direct influence coming from the soul. But his guilt is dissolved only once the soul of the person, whom he instigated into action by the projection of his thought energies, has forgiven him.

Similar things can result when a soul that is tied to a person through a common guilt incarnates. The inputs in the stars determine the path it takes so that it come together with its accomplice who is still a human being—perhaps for only a short period of life on Earth—in order to clear up their guilt together.

If the soul that is now in an earthly garment, a person, is furious, if he is still full of thoughts of hatred and revenge, wanting neither to forgive nor ask for forgiveness, that is, if he is still unrepentant, then it is possible—again through the active inputs which irradiate both instigator and perpetrator—that he cause negative energies to flow into the world of thoughts of the other person. In this way, he exerts a strong negative influence on the other, maneuvering him into misfortune and other wrongful deeds or even driving him to an early death by various ways and means—as long as the other one is within the deathspan of his life.

Since their inputs in the repository stars irradiate both instigator and perpetrator in order to stimulate them to forgiveness, which, however, does not take place, it is possible that the soul of the one who was driven to death again comes together with that soul that brought about its death, by incarnating anew within a period of some months or years. Both then meet up as human beings and by way of their correspondences will have their attention drawn to the fact that they have something to clear up with each other, and what it is. How we then behave toward each other is left to our free will.

The following course of events is also possible: A person can attract a soul in order to let himself be influenced by it or even to cause it to incarnate.

The course of events follows a similar lawful pattern: If a soul has the same or like predispositions as a person, the sending and receiving potential of both is similar. According to the principle of "like attracts like," we can, by emitting feelings and thoughts, easily attract souls that are near to Earth or souls to which we are bound or which are bound to us.

Within a "karma-association" of instigator, perpetrator and victim, more negative actions can take place over and over again, because the negative communications are already present. The mesh of guilt of such a, frequently quite extensive, circle of people and souls is often a tangled knot that would frighten us if we could see it.

In this way, people can influence other people as well as souls with the same or like ego aspects, for example, instigators, perpetrators and victims, visibly or invisibly, since like always fertilizes like.

For the sake of clarity, let us limit ourselves in this explanation to the relationship between instigator and perpetrator. Let us keep in mind that it makes no difference whether instigator and perpetrator knew each other personally in this or another life! This means that our share of guilt for occurrences concerning people and souls may be considerable without our knowing anything about it. However, our active correspondences, our pangs of conscience, perhaps even painful feelings of dismay and sorrow, signal to us that there is something in us that needs to be cleared up.

Perhaps we were once "merely" a brooding person, contemplating suicide, for instance. At that time, we may not have been aware of the fact that we emitted these thoughts and that these thoughts perhaps were the last drop of bitterness in a fellow person's cup of world-weariness, or self-pity, so that he took the step into death. And yet, we became guilty—perhaps many times over.

Of course, not only thoughts can act as instigators, but the written word as well. Especially writers, journalists and others that send out the spoken or written word into the world should be aware that they are responsible for every word and its effect on their fellow people. This also holds true for politicians, popes, ministers, priests and teachers—as well as for each one of us. Every thought, every word is energy and has its effect according to what it is filled with.

We live dangerously in the law of cause and effect, in the world of our correspondences! Moreover, from what has been stated, it also becomes clear that we can not only become a danger for many others, but also for ourselves, because everything that we cause, or sow—whether in feelings, sensations, thoughts, words or deeds—comes back to us.

Back to instigator and perpetrator. If the inputs become active, that is, if the repository stars in which the guilt of both is registered radiate into their souls, then this brings thoughts and the like into action in both of them, so that the soul in the beyond and the person on this side clear up the sins they have recognized. Whether both knew each other in this life makes no difference, because it is all about clearing up their own sinfulness.

How does a person now react in whom the repository stars have stimulated aspects of hatred, envy or compulsive physical urges, so that he may clear up the root of this evil with Christ and no longer do it?

The person who, in this example, may feel the flare-up of a desire to commit adultery—what does he do? Does he say to himself, "A correspondence, a cause, is calling my attention here. These surges of feelings want to tell me something. Today the strength is given to me to clear up a debt and to dissolve this negative impulse with Christ in order to free myself for higher things"? Or, does he nurture this sinfulness again, emitting accordingly? Then he may become an instigator again. Or does he even act upon it, committing adultery and creating a new binding?

If the soul of his partner in guilt, the previous instigator, is in the beyond at this point in time, then the person in whom the old passions, desires and compulsive urges became active again can intensely influence that soul—which is in the same world of desires, passions and compulsive urges— by sending, that is, telepathically, that it will suffer unendingly under the pressure of this influence, because the sins appear as pictures that cause it to suffer what it once did to others. The repository planets which radiate the inputs of both into their souls, can be the pathway for an early incarnation of the soul that is being targeted by the person. If under this influence the soul now incarnates, it may well be that it has to suffer heavily from the very beginning of its human life, because it incarnated with the active soul burden.

Through this process, a new binding is established: The soul of the person who induced the soul of its partner in guilt from the beyond to incarnate, by emitting the corresponding thoughts, is now bound even more tightly to the soul that incarnated too early.

These are only a few of the examples for the way threads are tied into knots in the immeasurably great web of our correspondences, or guilt.

In this way, an unimaginably knotted and entangled karma network may have developed, and continues to develop, which souls and human beings could never undo on their own. This is why the Son of God came into this world and became our Redeemer. He is the only one capable of freeing us from these entanglements, providing we want this, because each one of us has free will. We can become free by turning to Christ in us, in fervent prayer and with deep remorse, to ask for forgiveness—whether we know these people in this incarnation or not—and also by forgiving our neighbor who sinned against us, whether we know him or not. And if we no longer commit such or similar sins that were and are built up through our negative thoughts, words and actions, then Christ can undo this knotted network and we become free, if the other forgives us.

Let us once again become aware of the statement in the Bible that analogously says: "I tell you, on the day of judgment you will have to give account for every careless word you utter, for by your words you will be justified, and by your words you will be condemned." A "careless" word can be a word that is turned away from God, a hate-filled word, an envious thought or a compulsive wishful thought. Everything is energy. Nothing is ever lost. Whether positive or negative, it finds an echo in the person; for as a person calls into the canyon—into the world and into the cosmos—so will the echo come back in the same way.

How can we find our way out of external programming?

As long as we live our sinfulness to the full, we will be influenced and controlled by these, our correspondences. Once we become aware of this and begin very gradually to find our way out of this cycle of sinning and influencing our neighbor, in order to live more and more from the Spirit of God, we will understand ever more that for this path there is only one helper: Christ.

If we take one step toward Christ in us, by trying more each day to fulfill the commandments of God, then Christ will come several steps toward us. Only in this way do we find our way out of the straitjacket of our sins and gradually come into communication with our divine heritage. This is the liberation through our Savior, Christ.

A person who takes the steps toward Christ sows good thoughts and brings a good seed into the atmosphere through the principle "send good, receive good." From this good sending potential, good thoughts, good drops, can fall into the effervescing, egotistical, dangerous thoughts of a neighbor. A good drop, a good thought, can contribute to changing our neighbor's way of thinking so that he does not commit the dangerous deed he had already prepared. A good thought, a good drop, from the sending potential of a person who is striving toward God can stimulate a fellow person to not do something that otherwise might have ruined his whole life on Earth.

If we carry many external programs in us that we have expanded even more through our corresponding behavior, it will often be difficult to find the negative programs we brought with us into this life and those programs, our ego programs, that we created during this lifetime.

A person who is externally programmed, who is often controlled from without, should take himself back into his youth, back to an age he can still remember. Then, in a process of self-discovery, he should begin with the first programs he is aware of, in order to find out when and where this external programming in his life began. He should think back, reflecting on how it was implanted in him and what he made of it.

If he becomes aware of the programs from his youth, then he should recognize his wrongdoing from them, that is, he should clear up the sins he has recognized with the strength of Christ and no longer do them. If he seriously and conscientiously carries out this analysis of his life, it is possible that he may again find a part of the programs he brought with him into this lifetime. On the path of clearing up his sins, he can then also become aware, from the external programs, of those sins that he grafted onto these external programs.

Following the steps of our recognition, what is important is that we decidedly reprogram ourselves. Simply denying the old sinful programs is not enough. In order to become free and to find the self-reliance in our inner being, in our eternal self, we have to make a clear decision and set up new goals as well as the steps to reach them. If the new goals and values are principles of the laws of God, in the spirit of the Ten Commandments, the

Sermon on the Mount, or the commandment of love for God and neighbor, then these guidelines are support, orientation and a source of strength for us, because they are a part of our eternal divine being, which we unfold more and more by affirming and actualizing, by consistency and self-mastery.

*More links in the network of
sowing and reaping through espionage
for interest-groups of souls*

Within the network of sowing and reaping, there are countless entanglements and links, and we human beings, with our correspondences, our egoism, are always involved in them. The few descriptions given in this book should help us realize how close to us the forces of negativity, or even earth-bound souls are—and how cleverly they know to use our weaknesses in order to cause our downfall, and through us, the downfall of building the positive on Earth.

An example:

A group of people, an interest group—let's call them A—join together to develop a joint project, for instance, to further develop a machinery plant or the advancement of a firm. It is possible that in this group, one person merely seems to be of like mind, but wants to exploit the common interests of the group for himself in order to personally enrich himself from this joint venture. This seemingly interested person can be the listening post of an interest group of souls from the beyond—let's call them B—which, through the human listening post in group A, can find out what the interest group of souls can use for its own purposes.

It could be, for example, that through group B some information from group A should be smuggled into another firm or another interest group on Earth—let's call them C—which is close to the interest group B from the beyond. Perhaps the interest group from the beyond (B) and this the interest group on the Earth (C) have a common concern, for example, a joint plan to introduce a detailed genetic engineering project into the world, as a step toward the achievement of certain goals. Or, that the soul group (B) is interested in particularly promoting a certain large corporation, because then, according to their inputs which are already being activated via the planets, some souls from group B can incarnate again, and later be employed by the corporation and have the corresponding influence there to work for the achievement of certain interests.

At this point, it should be pointed out that such souls, which strive to interfere in the course of events in the world on Earth, are never souls with a higher consciousness, that is, of a higher degree of spiritual development. They are earth-bound souls, which do not turn their eyes heavenward, that is, they do not take the steps that lead to their divine heritage, but instead seek their well-being on the Earth, in the world. And the all-too-human on the Earth is not the divine, but the reversal of the divine, the negative. Therefore, no impulses for the higher development of humankind and for the good and the positive can be expected to come of these influences from the soul realms.

Therefore, souls can make use of human spies whose vibration is the same as their frequency, or whose souls belong to their conspiracy of souls. Such listening posts for the souls, also called spies for the souls, enable the souls to listen in on the interest group (A) on Earth. We already know the principle, "like attracts like." Each group, every community of people, or of souls, has a specific energy field with a specific vibration, or radiation. If an interest group on Earth, which is building a plant or wants to analyze the most diverse points essential for a positive purpose and expand on it together, has a higher vibration, a higher frequency, than those souls that want to influence things in the world to serve their own interests, then the souls have no access to the group on Earth. Since this energy field has a higher vibration, or radiation, than they do, the base souls also have no insight into it. Therefore, they often infiltrate such groups with a seemingly interested person whose soul vibration is the same as theirs, or whose soul is one of them. Through such a person of like vibration, they gain access on a vibrational level to this interest group (A). In this way, they create a channel, so to speak, a listening post, which can reach into this group on Earth.

The spy does not have to be aware that he is a spy. But from his dishonest motivation, which becomes clear to him in his feelings, sensations and thoughts and in his reactions, he can recognize that he can be used by the adversary, because the world of his thoughts, which forms his aura, is on the vibration level of the adversary. From the aura of the spy, the souls read what he has listened in on. In this way, he can become a traitor, a Judas, to the interest group (A) he was smuggled into.

What is quietly built up by the group on Earth (A) can then be channeled by the soul group, via the same or similarly vibrating instruments, or transmitter, as it were, into other people or other interest groups on Earth (B, C or D), perhaps for sabotage purposes. This self-serving hanger-on in group A is now tied to the souls and people in interest group A, which he has exploited for his own purposes. Only when group A has forgiven the spy, can God also forgive him. And only then, can the soul continue on its way. As long as there is no forgiveness, the network can continue to expand, becoming more and more dense and intertwined, when the person repeatedly does the same or like things.

We realize again and again that via the energy of the day, God is calling for our attention, showing us, reminding us and admonishing us. He gave us the Ten Commandments and the Sermon on the Mount; He gives us teachings and instructions. God and the divine beings knock on our conscience. However, neither God, the Eternal, whose children we are, nor the divine beings, whose brothers and sisters we are, will influence us. They merely admonish and remind us through our feelings, memories and thoughts, because God created us as fully responsible and mature children, and gave us free will to decide freely.

If we live in God, then according to the principle of "sending and receiving," the divine, the good, comes toward us. If we promote the negative, the sins, and if we attract negative forces via our sinfulness—likewise based on the principle of "sending and receiving"—then we will be influenced by our sins and the negative forces. As we have sown, so will we reap.

We should always make ourselves aware that without the help of the Christ of God we cannot come out of this network into which we have spun and continue to spin ourselves. This is why, for every person and for every soul, Christ is the Redeemer who helps us become free. On the path of clearing things up and actualizing the laws of God, we free ourselves from the network of our sins and return to the Father's house as the redeemed ones.

The number of "revolutions" of the human ego determines our earthly existence

Every body sounds and vibrates. The frequency rate of the body could be called the number of revolutions of the physical body.

Let us think of the motor of a vehicle: The body of the vehicle sounds according to the number of revolutions it makes. It is similar with the human body. Just as a person "revolves," so to speak, with his words and actions, in his world of feelings and thoughts, this is how he looks and behaves. The number of revolutions of the human ego determines the blows of fate and illnesses.

In today, a person determines his tomorrow. The person of today may again be the person of tomorrow, but with different physical features, exactly with the ones that he determined in a previous incarnation and that his soul brought again into another body. He is then marked by the active programs, by the vibration of his soul—by the number of "revolutions" of his soul.

The genetic make-up of a person always corresponds to the inputs in his soul, to the state of consciousness that the soul carries in the beyond and that it brings along into its incarnation. Its active programs and those that become active during the course of its life on Earth determine its earthly existence.

We should realize more often that what we take with us when we leave this world as a soul and do not clear up in the beyond, we will bring back into this side of life. We will then live as a human being in those places of this world where there are people who carry a part of our genes. It is also they who procreate our body, so that we are again with those people with whom we did not clear up in previous incarnations the things that needed to be cleared up at that time. In this life on Earth, we will again have an opportunity to clear it up.

There is a close interaction between soul and genes. Our genes not only connect us with our ancestors, with our "family tree." The burdens of our soul and resulting genetic make-up also bind us to those people whom we programmed in pre-vious incarnations, that is, with whom we had our way. Thus, the attraction between people goes way beyond the ancestral line.

It is not seldom that during a walk, while shop-ping, on the way to work, on the streets of this world, in general, we encounter people whom we either like or dislike. It is not only our thoughts, but mainly our feelings that give us information on what connects us to this person, or what binds us to them or even, for example, what they have moved in us in situations or occurrences of the past.

It is therefore not by chance that we look at this or that person who triggers an emotion in us or gets us thinking. The same or like vibrations have attracted us. They send and communicate with us. What attracts or repels us does not al-ways have to come from our neighbor. It is pos-sible that we were the one who implanted inputs in our neighbor in a previous incarnation, which begin to vibrate during this encounter and move the same or like things in us.

A person who watches himself and analyzes the thoughts and feelings that are stirred up in him at the moment of the encounter realizes what he should clear up in himself, that is, what he should transform, for example, from a base, disparaging vibration to a higher, unifying one. If our correspondences react and we do not pay attention to what stirs in us, then it may well be that we will meet this apparent stranger on the street again—if not during this earthly existence, then as a soul in the soul realms or in another incarnation. In another incarnation, he may then be our husband or wife, our child, a relative, a friend, a colleague or boss, depending on what aspects bind us. But today, we are given the chance to dissolve this binding, so that our soul and that of our neighbor can become free.

Each of us determines our tomorrow today. If we pay no attention to what upsets us, to what brings the world of our feelings and thoughts into turmoil, then this can be the seed for our tomorrow. We will again be faced with these irritations and similar feelings and thoughts, perhaps more strongly pronounced, more forceful and closer to home than today.

In this way, we increase and expand the potential of our correspondences, our sinfulness. It may shape the form of our body tomorrow, because what we look like in another existence will depend on the inputs that are then active in us. With this, we design our body, either with our good sides or with our sinfulness. And likewise holds true that whatever upset us today, what has marked us today, this is what we pre-determined for ourselves yesterday.

As a soul in the beyond, we will be no different than we are on this side of life, except that our body will be finer-material. The radiation of the soul is the garment of its incarnation. What is here on this side of life is also in the beyond. What corresponds to us today on this side of life also corresponds to us tomorrow in the beyond. Only the aggregate state changes from the coarse-material body into a finer substance, which we call soul. Our inputs, however, are the same, because just as the tree falls, so will it lie.

It is not only in our encounters with people that we experience our good sides and our correspondences, the sinfulness. When we see paintings or houses, flowers, stones, gardens and furnishings, down to the smallest objects—our good sides or even our correspondences, our sinfulness, can begin to vibrate.

Everything that we see or hear—for example, the song of birds, loud and shrill tones, disharmonious or harmonious music, and much, much more—helps us to find and recognize our own aura, our inputs, the positive as well as the negative. The same is true for smelling, tasting and touching. The combination of what we see, hear, smell, taste and touch—in connection with our world of feelings, sensations and thoughts—shows us who we really are.

There is a constant interaction between the world of our senses and of our feelings, thoughts, words and actions, our passions, desires, longings and the like. The world of our senses influences our positive as well as our negative aspects that are expressed in our behavior, which is our character portrait. Our behavior, in turn, influences the world of our senses. All these programs and communications make up our radiation, our aura. This means that the world of our senses, which was and is a decisive factor in shaping our behavior, our human character, stimulates our character traits again and again.

For us, this means that if we want to recognize our sinfulness, our personal law, our law of correspondence, in order to clear it up with the power of the Christ of God and no longer commit it, then we purify our soul and our senses. Or we give our stirrings free rein, that is, we continue to develop our negative character; and with this, we imprint our soul today, which tomorrow can be the form of our body.

Every one has the choice.

Our partner—our closest neighbor.
Building up and expanding the web of
bindings in marriage and partnership

During the course of his sojourn on Earth, every person experiences his own turning points in time, because our life on Earth is divided into timespans like the year with its seasons of spring, summer, autumn and winter. These phases during the course of a person's life correspond to the course of vital processes in his physical body. It runs in rhythms, which we could also call leaps in life. Whenever these leaps in time or life occur, the person's cast of mind changes in many ways; he crosses over into another world of thinking.

The transition from spring into summer of a life on Earth is called puberty; a child matures into adulthood, into a man or a woman. The growing young person leaves behind spring, the uncomplicated and free life, the security of his parents' home. According to his own criteria, he builds a new life for himself with totally different feelings, words and actions. Thus, he passes into summer with everything he has learned and acquired until then.

In nature, the transition from spring into summer brings once again an increased flow of sap in the plant world, so that blossoms and the first fruits appear on the trees, which will then ripen during the summer. With us human beings it is similar. Especially during the transition from puberty into adulthood, the energies intensely rise again, which, among other things, bear the desire for the propagation of life. We have often reversed these lawful forces that serve the preservation and propagation of life. We transformed down the principle of creating and giving life—by reversing it into wanting to have and to take—into sexuality, which is oriented toward gaining pleasure.

Just as nature is active in bringing forth the fruit that corresponds to the respective species, the young person, too, becomes more and more active to enter into a twosome relationship, so that the drive for life can bring forth its fruit, which, from the viewpoint of purity, means that the branch on the tree of life wants to bear fruit, that is, children.

Therefore, procreating children would be what nature intended. Since most souls that are now incarnated, that is, human beings, carry within themselves from previous lives the desire for reproduction in its reversed form, the desire for sexuality, sexuality for its own sake, as it were, increases more and more. This means that the physical act is ultimately abused. Only one fruit or none at all may be produced, one child or two at the most. But sexuality, which one can also call a brief means of relaxation, remains.

Sexuality for its own sake is playing with the forces that are given for the creation of life and not for play, for senseless waste. During a sexual exchange, a sensual tension is deliberately built up which then discharges itself in a "sensory overload." In this, the man as well as the woman lose an enormous amount of physical and soul energy. The climax of the physical act is then felt as relaxation.

Living as a human being in our world brings much tension, situations of pressure and failure, stress and annoyance, the nervous system comes into tension and vibration. Frequently, a counterbalance, relaxation, is sought in sexuality. But since the collapse of the stimulation of the nerves, the induced relaxation, does not bring with it the solution to what led to the excessive strain on the nerves, the causes remain, tension builds up again and with it, the desire for sexual relaxation. Therefore, in order to relax in the act of sexuality, the man takes the woman and the woman takes the man.

If we bring it down to a single denominator, one can say: Man and woman often enter into a "pairship" in order to "master their life together" in this way. If they are compatible in their sexual love, that is, if they are one in their physical relationship, then, by way of sending and receiving, a communication field, a vibration field, is produced from many energies like desires, longings, expectations and the like that vibrate from the one to the other. This communication field is exciting in a human way, and is called infatuation or love.

Moreover, in this drive for stimulation, pleasure and relaxation, the woman sees in the man, and the man in the woman, some essential aspects that they like but do not possess themselves. They find these aspects in the other wonderful and useful as a possible contribution to a marriage.

And all this is then called "love." Both think this has to be enough for the happiness that one expects from the other. Then man and woman either give each other a pledge for their lifetime on Earth and marry before civil authorities or a priest or minister, or they are content with living together in a so-called partnership.

This "pairship," in which two people are closely involved with one another, begins, whether it is called marriage or partnership. Each expects something from the other—and neither wants to give too much, for they think that love should be the mechanism by which they are complemented in every way. Perhaps they do indeed complement each other for some years in sexuality, but in those attributes that the one should contribute to the other—that is, provide a service—it becomes more and more difficult. The first difference of opinion begins, and in this way, quarreling draws into the marriage or partnership. Often unplanned, a child was conceived through their world of sexual desires, so that one or several children become a part of their growing incompatibility.

One now reproaches the other because the latter does not do this or that, for example, not fulfilling what the other expected before the marriage. Suddenly, a great many different correspondences appear, with which both may have bound themselves to each other in a previous life, and which have now led them together again. Instead of dissolving these correspondences, these links in the network of cause and effect, they continue to quarrel, because suddenly they see each other quite differently, namely, with the eyes of the law of their correspondences.

The disagreements grow worse and the desire for physical relations diminishes, because they no longer get along, since the halo from the expectations and desires of the one that was spun around the other has dissolved. Thus, so-called love is shattered.

The active correspondences now direct their eyes and their drives. By the eyes, one or the other is then driven to another mate, first secretly and then officially. In this way, a separation is pre-programmed. The children are hit especially hard. Either they are pushed out of the way or left with one of the parents. Until this step is taken, it may take years of constant pushing and pulling. The bindings, the correspondences, call out loud; they want to be resolved. Until the moment when they are finally pushed to the side unresolved, many more correspondences and bindings are formed.

From time to time the objection is heard, "With us, in our marriage or partnership, it is different." It can be they have cleared things up with each other and become steadfast in themselves, so that they walk side by side without expecting anything from the other. Then it may be that they just complement each other in their development to higher ethics and morals. But it is also possible that they have stopped talking with each other because they don't have anything more to say to each other. Through this, a semblance of peace is upheld. Television programs and gossip may then be the subject of their conversations. They have managed to come to an arrangement in their correspondences. Or both have accepted the other's habits; in a certain sense, projections are "equalizers." There may then be an external "peace."

Every one searches for love and finds it solely in God.

Meanwhile, the person has moved into the summer of his life without bearing good fruits, the fruits of the actualization of the commandments of God. In the school on Earth in which he finds himself, every person is called upon to clear up with others what bothers him in the other person. Whatever upsets him is a part of his correspondences, of his sinfulness, that he ought to clear up with the other one in order to free himself from the sins that bind him to his neighbor, for example, to his partner. With his next great leap in time, or in life, when a person gradually moves from summer into autumn, that is, into the middle of his life, he senses that his life is declining, like the crown of a tree when it bears many fruits.

A person who does not bear good fruit because he cannot get along with his neighbor in his feelings, thoughts, words and actions—be it in marriage, partnership or within a community framework, but also at work—will begin to panic. This panic, which comes from the active world of his desires, from fear of having missed out on something, again contains further intense desires and longings: for example, the wish to experience sex more, the longing to have another partner who, wrongly presumed, will have all those abilities and attributes which the previous partner did not have.

Until now, life did not bring this person what he had wished and imagined for himself. He hardly ever asks himself what the reason for this might be, because it is obvious and clear to him: It already began in his childhood; it was his parents' and teachers' fault. His friends, too, were not as they should have been. His marriage partner promised more than was kept, disappointingly so—thus, a complete wash-out. At work, too, not everything turned out as it had appeared in the beginning. His boss and colleagues think only of themselves and do not value his qualities as would be fitting. Therefore, the desire awakens to change jobs in order to earn more and climb higher on the ladder of success; or the decision grows to leave a community in order to talk big somewhere else, to peddle his opinions and to finally realize his ambitious plans for playing a leading role there.

Such life-changing decisions are therefore caused by that sense of panic that indicates that he has not made good use of the summer of his life. He produced hardly any healthy, good-tasting fruit, because he did not clear up his correspondences with his partner, those things that had mutually attracted them and to which they are bound. At work, his existing abilities were neither developed nor expanded, because the quarreling that prevailed in his marriage and partnership was also reflected at work. The disagreements in marriage and partnership led to disagreements at work, because as a result of the disagreements, the quality of his work left something to be desired. And so, he began to quarrel at work, making plain the desire to improve his situation in another job, to leave a community, because one cannot get along with the people there—and not least, a divorce from his partner has been announced.

A person who has insight into the most varying situations in the life of a person knows that this lifespan of reorientation and the attempt for a new beginning can start at the age of thirty years and end between forty and fifty years, when panic sets in because the person has hardly brought forth any fruit during the summer of his life. He had to recognize that his life until now has brought him no meaningful fulfillment, only squabbling and job changes. A person hardly ever admits to this. He usually explains his failures with the fact that things did not work out in his marriage or partnership, and he often decides to start a new relationship. One doesn't need to be a prophet to see that this new partnership or relationship will not work out either, because a person always keeps seeking his own correspondences and what lies in the world of his desires, which others should fulfill for him.

The same is true at work and in the community. A person who does not know what he wants will be driven, from one flower, from one partner, to the other, from one job to the next, and from one community to the next. We can change our shirt as much as we like; we will still always put on the same shape and color.

As long as we are not true to ourselves and do not develop our spiritual self, our true self, we will always expect from our neighbor what we do not have, and therefore, cannot give. As long as we do not develop our spiritual self, we will not find stability, but will always be on the lookout for people, jobs and communities that we think will be able to give us what, in the end, we do not have and do not want to develop.

In the autumn of our life, we then stand there with empty hands, but with an extensive negative experience, with a network of countless knots and threads that we will have to untangle, either as souls in the spheres of purification or in further incarnations.

A person who does not bear ripe fruit, who has not used his summer years, will not be self-possessed during his autumn years, but will be a childish old man who looks back upon his humanly spectacular earthly existence that he talks about whenever possible, in order to perhaps gain recognition from some younger person for his wild activities, which did not bear the good fruits of love for God and neighbor, but only the "me, me, me" in the network of feelings, longings, passions, compulsions and flightiness from one to another, from one job to another, from one community to another. What is left? An emptiness, an unfulfilled life, an aged existence that revolves around itself. Just as it was during his spring and summer, so is it now, too, in autumn.

In just one single life on Earth, we can—with the help of Christ—untie many knots and dissolve many threads in the web of our correspondences—if we consistently follow a higher goal, if we heed the impulses of the energy of the day and make use of the chances that our life offers us each day. However, in one single incarnation we can also considerably expand the web of our sinfulness. Especially our partner is close to us—within the law of sowing and reaping. He is our "closest neighbor," so to speak, in a very special way. If we resolve with him what needs to be resolved, then the grace of God will dissolve many other threads of guilt and binding—if our neighbor forgives us. We know that if we take one step toward Christ by doing what He called us to do, He comes several steps toward us.

Excuses ...
Whoever keeps the commandments
of God gains farsightedness and
develops the love and wisdom of God

Every person, no matter of what religion, even an atheist or anti-Christian, is called upon by the commandments of God to recognize these and apply them in his daily life, so that his soul may be purified and enter its divine heritage again, the all-encompassing eternal law of love and wisdom.

We people have many excuses why we have done and do this or that, why we belong to a church institution, why we believe or don't believe, why we see this commandment one way, and then another way, why we doubt in God or believe in His existence, why we talk about the "mysteries of God" and about the "punishing and chastising God" or why we believe in a God of love and wisdom, and why, despite all this, we continue to sin.

All, but really all, sinful human ways are null and void before the face of God. Only one thing is important: To fulfill the commandments of God that He gave us through Moses and the Sermon on the Mount that Jesus taught and personified. At the end of His Sermon on the Mount, Jesus said, "Every one who hears these words of Mine and does them is like a wise man who built his house on a rock ... And every one who hears these words of Mine and does not do them is like a foolish man who built his house on sand."

Thus, we are called to fulfill the commandments of God, part of which is also the Sermon on the Mount of Jesus, no matter what opinions, conceptions, theories and maxims we may have. We cannot get around recognizing our sins, clearing them up and no longer doing them.

The person who takes the step into the actualization and fulfillment of the divine, that is, the person who leaves the old tracks of all-too-humanness in order to dare to be with God gains far more than he leaves behind. The active Christian, who has made this decision and has set out on this new path, can say from his own experience: It is well worth it to make God the center of one's life and His commandments the guiding principles for one's actions. For the one who keeps the commandments of God gains farsightedness and ever more insight into the great laws of the love and wisdom of God. And then he no longer needs to theorize and philosophize about God; he no longer needs to peddle his opinions about how God is or should be. Moreover, he will no longer talk about the "mysteries of God," because more and more things become evident to the purified soul and the cleansed person. He looks into the depths that are unfathomable to the one who is surrounded by the veils of his ego.

The one who does not open the kingdom of the inner being has no insight into the eternal law and no access to the kingdom of the inner being. As a result, he introduces the "mysteries" and the "inscrutable counsel" of God into his concept of what God is.

Thus, we are on Earth to open up our divine heritage, the love and wisdom, so that our senses may perceive what is in all things: God. And then, our feelings, thoughts, words, actions and works are drenched with sun by God. That is life. Everything else is vegetating, mere opinion and conception, an inflated shadow existence in a shadow box, where each one wants to be the greatest with his theories and interpretations.

The wise, luminous person with a high soul radiation and a refined body structure

Wise people are spiritualized, sun-drenched people, as it were, who are in communication with the inner light. The soul of a spiritualized person is purged to a high degree and his body is cleansed from the dross of the sinful ego. He is balanced and a master of his own thoughts.

A luminous soul also has a high soul radiation. The effect is a high body vibration even if it shows the traces of what the soul brought along into its life on Earth, that is, the basic equipment of its physical body. During the course of its life on Earth, this basic equipment can become finer or coarser in structure and radiation, depending on the way the individual thinks and lives.

If the person turns to the spiritual-divine life by fulfilling the laws of God step by step, then the vibration of his soul and body refines. The soul that is becoming more and more pure attains a higher vibration, which also permeates the physical body and raises it to a rate of vibration that transcends the traces of the previous burden.

Wise people are luminous, enlightened people, as it were, who have conquered their sins with the power of Christ, the inner light. Through the fulfillment of the commandments of God, that is, through a life of tolerance, good will, respect for neighbor and rendering honor to God, the five senses of the person become clear. Through the power of Christ, the sinfulness, which is expressed in one's feeling, thinking, speaking, acting, wanting and wishing, is transformed into the will of God. This means that the person fulfills the will of God more and more.

In inner Christianity, the Christianity of the deed, of the fulfillment of the divine commandments, the path to the heart of God is as follows:

According to the commandments of God, put your life in order in your thinking, feeling and wanting, and in so doing, pave the way into heavenly order with the help of the Christ of God in you.

People of inner Christianity live in active faith. They strive to transform their self-will into the will of God through self-recognition, by repenting of the sins they have recognized, by attaining forgiveness and forgiving, by making amends and by no longer doing the sin that was recognized and cleared up.

A Christian of the deed cleanses his soul and his physical body of sin, of the dross of his egoism, as it were, so that the inner light can turn the ever more purged five senses into organs of perception for those things that the sinful senses cannot perceive. The five senses are then no longer blinded by sin.

People who are in this state of enlightenment no longer judge and condemn. The person who has attained this state of divine communication, of inner perception, sees deeper and hears from the words of his fellow people what they do not want to reveal, but which nevertheless, resonates. The purified senses of smell, taste and touch, as well, are directed toward the inner perception.

Through the refinement of the interaction between senses and thoughts, words and actions, the person attains this afore-mentioned ability to perceive which, in the course of his further enlightenment, gives him ever more insight into what other people merely dream about—into the principles of the law that are in matter, that is, that take place in the physical world. Moreover, such a person attains communication with the subtler cosmic forces, all the way to the pure Being. By opening the inner perception, his neighbor is an open book for him, since each person reveals himself in many different ways, whether he wants to or not.

In few words, this is the gradual opening of the inner being, of the divine heritage.

The correlation between an outer posture and an inner bearing.
Correspondences and weaknesses that lie hidden behind striking a pose

Every posture of the body discloses the inner attitude, the strength and spiritual development of a person. An undisciplined body posture indicates a lack of order in the thinking of an individual and indicates his self-will.

This is merely to touch on a few common features of body postures that are particularly widespread in the western world.

Many Europeans occasionally strike up a pose. For example, when sitting, the body is bent way forward or nonchalantly back, or the arms are kept folded or the legs crossed. According to the divine laws, these so-called "poses for show" mean that the person wants to hide his disorder and his self-will, letting his intellect more or less play itself out by showing off in order to hide his insecurity. Such postures of ours also indicate that we belittle our fellow people in order to enhance ourselves. This means that we need this enhancement, because we have neither order nor steadfastness in our lives, and thus, no wisdom either.

Such postures show exactly where our correspondences lie, for example, in the levels of correspondence of the laws of Order, Will or Wisdom. These three levels of correspondences, also called soul garments, shape the outer appearance of a person. The afore-mentioned external postures indicate an impure and burdened inner bearing, correspondences that lie in these three soul garments.

People with such postures have contrived certain thinking patterns, because they are very insecure in their private and professional lives. For this reason, they cling to their concepts, to their thought patterns and, at the same time, to their own body. These postures also expose the pessimist, who knows everything better, who value-judges and denigrates everything that does not fit into his scheme of thought.

The folded arms and crossed legs indicate arrogance and, at the same time, insecurity and indecisiveness.

A person who strikes these compulsive poses of holding on to himself wants to hide, among other things, his inhibitions, his weaknesses and inadequacies. Inhibitions and weaknesses always indicate ignorance and arrogance. People with these postures speak in a different way than they think. They can talk about love and kindness and good will, and yet their thoughts are totally opposed to these.

Here, we need to take into account the fact that such expressions as "arrogance," "indecisiveness," "pessimism" and the like contain different accentuations and values for each individual person. These then find different expressions, be it only in nuances, in the corresponding posture.

The weaknesses that are expressed in these poses can also be the typical "good little boy" or "good little girl" attitude. Whoever shows no sign of any greater inner and outer values will flatter others in order to look good.

People with a high degree of actualization see through their neighbor.
They work with the inner strength

I f we want to recognize our neighbor, we have to explore ourselves first, according to the words of Jesus in the following sense, "First take the beam out of your own eye, and then you will see clearly to take the splinter out of your brother's eye." This means that we should first watch ourselves, how *we* act, how *we* treat our fellow people, what *our* body postures, that is, our poses, are like.

A person who has explored himself and overcome his negativity also knows how to interpret the splinter in his neighbor's eye. He will then be able to see what really lies behind the postures of his fellow people. Based on his experiences in overcoming his human baseness, he will, however, no longer feel and think in an evaluating or judgmental way. Even in turbulent situations, he will remain impersonal, that is, he will remain in balance.

Therefore, we must learn to see and to hear, which means to read from what we see and hear what is going on in us, where we are indecisive, why we hold on to our body or why we have this or that so-called habit. A habit is an aspect of our character; it is our imprinting, a behavior pattern, imprinted by the world of our thoughts and feelings, which also shapes our body. Only once we have worked our way through the jungle of our own show-off programs, and, through self-recognition, have cleared up, or largely cleared up, our world of sinful programs with the help of Christ, are our senses of sight and hearing purified to the extent that we make no false diagnoses or prognoses; nor do we let ourselves be deceived by external behavior patterns that are forced—even when people make believe and outwardly take up a correct posture. Whatever has not grown naturally appears cramped. In the company of others, such a person's way of talking and his whole behavior is much more contrived than if he were to just be himself.

Very little remains hidden to a wise person who has vanquished his self with the help of the inner Christ of God, that is, who has overcome his grave negative characteristics and refined his character. He has learned to perceive the total impression of his fellow people. From this total impression, the details, the nuances of a given behavior then speak to him, which, on account of his own actualization, he is then able to interpret correctly and in accordance with the law of divine Order, divine Will and divine Wisdom.

People who have largely overcome their grave sins with the help of the Christ of God, on the basis of the Ten Commandments and the Sermon on the Mount, are open and upright people; they are masters of their own thoughts.

Open people have a pure character and therefore, also a relaxed, upright body posture. Their walk is upright; their steps are firm; their body shows no signs of swaying or wavering, but firmness of character. Such a person sits upright; both feet are on the ground, because he is down to earth. His hands rest quietly in one another or plain and simply in his lap. His look is open for all people and for everything that comes toward him.

People who have found their way to their innermost being have nothing to hide—they are at one with the transcendent power, the Spirit of the Christ of God, who leads and guides them. A person who does not mark himself with the stamp of affected openness, but has truly matured from within, also has spiritual insight and enlightenment. Every forced posture can be recognized from a person's radiation, because whatever has not grown is merely put on, and what is put on gives a coarse impression.

If the spiritual attitude grows from within to without, the person is relaxed, light, vibrant, open, orderly and conscientious. People who have oriented their life to the highest source, God, not only have an open look, but also a corresponding attitude of the spirit. They are disciplined and people of the deed, who work with the inner forces and see with the eyes of wisdom. They see through their fellow people and solve the situations of daily life with the forces of the Spirit of God.

Every person is on Earth in order to transform himself from sinner to the blessed one—whether we believe in it or not. Sooner or later, we will all learn that only when we go through the eye of the needle of our own self-conquest with Christ, will we attain a flawless character, become God-conscious and close to God.

Poses of self-deception

Other features of our self-deception particularly characterize us in the western world. We have the habit—and this is again an expression of our character—of resting our elbows either on our thighs or on the edge of a table, often in order to hold our head with both hands. Or we cross our legs and rest an elbow on a leg, holding our chin in our hand. In this way, we try to support our body.

The person who has worked on the beam in his own eye can, since he has worked on himself, deduce the inner attitude of his neighbor from his external posture. In general, these poses indicate an indolence of the mind, negligence and a tepid soul. Such people are often of a brooding nature, who dissect and talk to death the things and statements of others. This "dis-attitude" corresponds to the disorder, self-will and intellect of such persons. These body poses also characterize the opinion leader, the opinion maker, who rarely tolerates another view. Because of the indolence of his mind, he will make hasty judgments, thus condemning his fellow people. Indolence does not allow time to seriously think about a matter. It drapes its own opinion over it, which is then regarded as the truth for a lazy and superficial person.

It is precisely this attitude that shows many attributes of egotism and disorder in daily life. Lazy people are negligent people, who stubbornly insist on their own ideas and opinions, fiercely defending them. Such types of people quickly reach a personal judgment, creating "their own" image of others that they then often defend, fanatically.

People with this attitude can join the ranks of cholerics and fanatics, but likewise pessimists. Because of their tepid disposition and effeminate soul, they mostly do not have the strength to overcome, in due course, the things and fate at hand. As a result of the weakness of their mind, they keep bringing up things long since past, in order to draw attention to themselves. They try to gain the favor of others in order to bask in their light and revel in the appreciation of others.

Much talking, gesticulating, fidgeting—everything betrays us

Other general features that can be observed especially in the western world—but also in other cultures—are a lot of thoughtless talking, gesticulating and fidgeting with any small object within reach, for example, a pencil, pen, ruler and the like.

People who say a lot of unessential things are mostly insecure, unstable people who don't really know how to live and act correctly. They lack concentration and are torn apart in their world of feelings. Their lack of concentration results in insecurity that they try to cover up with many words. They talk and talk and, in the end, don't know themselves what they have said and thus achieved. Asked what their concern is or what they wanted to express, they mostly begin all over again to say the same thing.

Such torn people are also tedious and circuitous workers. They know how to tackle a job, but seldom finish it. If at all possible, they will parcel out their work and lay it on other people's shoulders, while talking and fidgeting a lot, only to finally hand over the work. All the while they still put themselves in the limelight, explaining how burdened they are and giving detailed instructions about how the other one should organize and perform the tasks that were assigned.

The personality of such types is shaped by their past. Their egocentric character quotes the past over and over again in the present, thus bringing it to life again. Such types of people have great difficulty to forgive. What was once done to them or what they think someone did to them—that is, things of the past that offended them—they often hold on to in their subconscious for years, even decades. At a given time, they call it up and state it, perhaps to implant feelings of guilt in the people in question, even if outwardly they appear to be loyal and sincere.

Whatever is served up again and refreshed from the past, from the subconscious and conscious mind, will fall back to where it came from, but considerably enlarged as a result of these further activities of thought. Since, in this way, the conscious mind and subconscious fill more and more with pictures of identical or similar content, the disposition of the person reacts ever more strongly the more he thinks about the same or like things. This may make him choleric and aggressive. The person reacts reproachfully toward his environment. A strongly agitated subconscious and conscious mind influence the nervous system more intensely. This causes this type of person to talk more and more; folk wisdom says, "He talks with his hands and feet." All this talking and gesticulating marks the person's facial expressions and his whole body. Such types of people are domineering and have an inflated character. Often, the shape of their body is similar.

The outer appearance of a person is always an expression of his inner condition. The mass of the body, too, is a reflection of inner processes. A thin, almost emaciated body often indicates excessive egocentricity and stinginess. A voluminous body shows gluttony and revelry. For such a person, hardly anything is good enough. He lets himself go and indulges in eating and drinking, in all the sensual pleasures offered to him, be it in the craving for food or drink or in excessive sensuality. Both the thin person as well as the obese type of person are disposed toward easily slipping into compulsiveness, and even into excesses and acts of violence.

The person who does not conquer himself will sooner or later be defeated by his own inputs, the causes, his own personal law that is the law of his correspondences.

The beholding one sees behind his neighbor's mask.
The one who lives conscious of God can be guided by the inner light more and more

Because the external behavior influences the inner being, the soul and person, and the inner being, in turn, expresses itself externally, the person portrays himself at every moment.

The wise person who rests in God registers all these features of his fellow people. He sees how the behavior of his fellow people changes, their facial expression, their features and gestures. He sees the refinement or coarsening of the body and also registers the individual expressions of the body of the different types of people. For the wise person, every person is a barometer, from which he can read what the person really thinks and who he really is. Thus, he sees through his fellow people. But from this knowledge, he passes on only as much as can be helpful for his neighbor.

He sees the yes-man and the tyrannical person, the pompous and the hypocritically humble. He sees behind the mask of sweet words and smiles; he recognizes the signs and causes of bitterness. He sees through every gesture, every facial expression. He knows how to interpret every little wrinkle and sees and hears what the other one does not see and hear.

The expression of the whole body supplies countless information to the beholding one. He knows what the one wants to express with his torrent of words and why another is silent. He knows why the one is strong and the other unstable, because in the symptoms, he perceives the person's characteristics that lie behind his outer form of appearance. He knows why this one has a short and the other an even breathing rhythm. He knows the symptoms that might trigger suffering and illness. But he seldom speaks about it, because according to the laws of God, freedom of will is an inviolable commandment.

People who strive toward the inner Christianity, the inner religion, live in active faith. With the power of the Christ of God, they live and work according to His commandment, "Do to others as you would have them do to you." Or, "What you do not want others to do to you, do not do to them." Through this, they draw closer to the inner light, God's love.

People who think and live in this consciousness monitor their words, their gestures, their whole behavior. The one who turns to inner discipline, to order in his life, who speaks only what is essential expresses only what is most important and does it in such a way that it can be understood and accepted. For this reason, his words are borne by the law of God, by the divine Will, which makes one free and which allows others their free will so that they, too, can unfold according to their own nature.

The person who has his words and behavior under control knows what he is saying. He has explored and experienced it on and in himself in the right way. With an upright posture and an open look he states objectively and consciously, in a straightforward manner, what he himself has experienced, worked out and lived through. The honesty and openness of the person who keeps the commandments of God more and more each day fills him with inner calm, security and stability. This is the expression of inner stillness. God reveals Himself in the stillness.

People of an upright, God-conscious character have mostly gone through a hard school in life. They took things as they came, compared them to the Ten Commandments and the Sermon on the Mount and lived according to the divine laws they had recognized.

It would be blasphemous to think that a human being is able to direct the fate of this world and to comprehend the universe, the All. The person who strives toward the love for God and neighbor and toward God's wisdom is aware that there is a supreme Intelligence, which guides all things, including the fate of the universe, the All. People who are aware of this supreme Intelligence that permeates and directs the entire universe, and which is the immutable law, will endeavor each day to think, speak and act according to the Commandments of God, so that they may be led and guided by the highest Intelligence, God.

On the path of the spiritualization of our
soul and the illumination of our person,
we find our way into the divine law
of consonance, into the unity
and communication with God

The person who has attained spiritual knowledge and the resulting fulfillment from it knows the workings of the law of reversal, the law of correspondence.

The law of correspondence may also be called the law of reversal, because all those who think, speak and act with their sinfulness, their correspondences, have reversed the law of God. They turned the love of God into self-love, the will of God into self-will, the divine Self into selfishness, peace into discord, harmony into disharmony and the like.

The person who actualizes and fulfills the law of God knows from his own experience that all that goes out from a person will also come back to him. Therefore, the person who accepts the law of correspondence is aware that all ungodly ways of thinking, speaking and acting will return to the sender. The echo shows this: Whatever we call into the canyon is what the echo brings back to us.

We will continue to expose ourselves to the law of karma, "what you sow, you will reap," until we—each and every one of us—transform in the light of Christ our personal law, our correspondences, on the path of remorse, of clearing up our sinfulness and of the do-no-more. Through this, soul and person gradually immerse in God's love. The soul then comes into its divine heritage; it opens the powers of heavenly Order, of the Will of God, of divine Wisdom; it again makes the Earnestness of the spirit being its own, as well as Patience, which is kindness, the Love and the Mercy, which is gentleness, of the Eternal.

The seven basic powers of God are the eternal law and are the divine heritage of our pure spiritual body. We human beings are on Earth to develop these seven basic powers of God, the divine heritage of every pure being, that is, to uncover them and apply them. This is the path of every soul, whether discarnate or incarnate, whether we are there as a soul, or here as a human being. None of us can avoid opening up again what our soul possesses eternally: to be divine.

If a person turns toward the commandments of God, which are excerpts from the divine law, by recognizing his sins, by repenting, clearing them up and doing them no more, he will apply and fulfill the laws of God more and more. Through this step-by-step fulfillment of the principles of the law of God, soul and person, but principally the soul, will attain the law of consonance, which says: In those aspects where the soul is filled by the holy and eternal law and is connected with the eternal law, it is also in consonance with God, the love and wisdom, in equality and thus, in communication.

The divine communication is the All-communication, because God is present in all things. It also includes the purification planes and this Earth. When we human beings clear up our sinfulness with the help of the Christ of God and no longer do it, then we gradually open up the

All-communication and enter into communication with our origin, the love and wisdom of God. Then we gradually become wise, because we open ourselves to the all-permeating divine stream, to God, whose children we are.

Let us bring to mind again that base thinking, feeling and wanting is active in the law of cause and effect, in the law of sowing and reaping. This is turning away from God and the consonance, in the correspondences with the same and like sinners. This is the equality in the causal law. To the extent that the soul cleanses itself from the burden of sin, it is spiritualized and the person enlightened. It is in this way that we find our way into the divine law of consonance, into the unity and communication with God. To the extent that the person fulfills the laws of God, the soul of the person attains this consonance, becoming one with the mighty Spirit of love and wisdom, with the Creator-Spirit in the nature kingdoms and in the All, the universe.

The person who has attained this consonance with the power of God keeps order in his life and lives in moderation. He is open, straightforward, just and loving. Just as he is *for* God, so is he also *for* his neighbor and *for* the nature kingdoms. He is aware that he is a cosmic being, a being of the All, because he knows about his divine heritage, in which he finds himself more and more.

People with this consciousness are not enthusiasts, unworldly or dreamers; they are not turned away from the world, but toward it. They are in the world, but are not with the negative, the non-divine, in the world.

The law of correspondence envelops the truth and narrows a person's field of vision—to his own well-being, to himself

The glorious, immutable and eternal law of God brings all of us into consonance with God, the love and freedom, and uncovers our divine heritage for us. Through this, we gain insight into all the outer and inner processes, into the divine law and into the law of envelopment, the law of correspondence.

The longing of the soul that strives toward God and of a God-conscious person knows only one goal: to become one with God, the eternal law. A wise person increasingly unveils his soul through the fulfillment of the commandments of God. He has turned toward God and has largely overcome his personal law, the law of correspondence. He has unveiled himself and reflects the law of truth, which is love and wisdom.

The law of correspondence envelops the truth and thus, the soul and the person as well. The result is a narrowed field of vision in the person, because egotistical thinking and acting have enveloped the truth. The connection to one's neighbor is cut off in this way. The egoist revolves more and more around himself. What he does not have—love, wisdom, freedom, happiness, security—he demands from his neighbor. On a small scale, this attitude of expectation has led and still leads to quarreling and fighting, and on a large scale, through statesmen, to war and annihilation of other cultures, cities and countries.

Through this reversal, the envelopment of soul and person, the person is oriented only to himself and often has eyes only for his own well-being. One's own well-being excludes the common good, and thus, the seven basic powers, the divine heritage, as well, which is no longer recognized by the egoist, since he looks only to his own envelopment, his plasma—also called aura—which, in turn, reflects to him only his own wishes, passions, his whole egotistical behavior. The mirror of his egoism is his aura, his plasma, the radiation image that reflects his own inputs in color and form.

Whether the person wants it or not, he is marked by his own inputs and thus, gives himself away. Many a one can embellish much with words, but they cannot change their own radiation image with this.

Christ offered and still offers us help for self-help. He is the help. But we human beings, who have the free will to decide freely for or against Christ, determine ourselves whether we want to accept Christ's help or not. We accept it by recognizing every day, in the upsurge of our correspondences, what corresponds to our all-too-human person, our base nature, by clearing it up with Christ's help and by no longer committing these sins. However, we also have the freedom to turn away from Christ by continuing to sin.

If we decide for the help of the Christ of God, we will also call on Him in our inner being for help. With this call to Christ for help and the firm will to no longer commit our sins, the help of Christ for self-help can begin.

Help for self-help means that we ourselves must become active, so that Christ's help can become effective. We must take a step toward Him, so that He can come several steps toward us. Just the faith in Christ and the knowledge of His power are of little use for us if we do not recognize and clear up our sinfulness, so that His power in us can become active for us, and transform our shadows into light.

How a person's world of programs develops

The following facts and correlations—about the development and use of our world of programs, about the function of our five senses and the possibility to recognize and clear up correspondences in the world of our feelings, sensations, thoughts, words and deeds—have already been explained in the first chapters of this book, even if from a different angle and not so thoroughly. These repetitions are to give a deeper understanding.

Our soul came into this world and took on a body that it put in good working order for this life. First and foremost, imprinting and perception take place via the senses. On this basis, the life programs for this Earth were and are gradually developed, programs of use and instruction, as it were, for the body during its earthly existence. The first programs of perception are formed by seeing, hearing, smelling, tasting and touching. At the same time, the physical body programs itself to be able to walk and move. Then, very gradually, the soul develops the programs for speech and communication via the physical body, and then follow the programs for learning, for experience, for an occupation and further programs that we need for our life on Earth as human beings. In the further course of our life on Earth, we graft programs of sin onto our programs of life and instruction, for example, ambition, egocentricity, envy, enmity, intolerance, disparagement of others, self-enhancement, falseness, deception, lying, fraud and much more.

And the sinfulness in the soul, which corresponds to the inputs in our genes, gradually stirs in the young person. To remove or weaken these first negative programs, parents and teachers should be good role models. If this does not happen, then such inputs from earlier incarnations will come to fruition in the child, gradually shaping the person and becoming noticeable as newly grafted sinful programs.

We act and react with this world of our programs, whereby our reactions are decisive in our being able to explore ourselves in them and recognize what the life programs and perception programs are or what is sinful. As soon as a child can tell good from evil, parts of its sinful programs become active. If this is not heeded during the early years, the person begins to expand these active programs or parts of them via his feeling, sensing, thinking, speaking and acting. If the person does not know why he is on Earth—namely, to recognize his sinful programs, to clear them up with Christ's help and to no longer do them— then the sensory programs and programs of use and instruction for the body will mix with the programs of sin. As already mentioned, we can then speak of a mixing board of programs. The person's whole behavior then becomes a mixture that originates from the mixing board of programs in our conscious mind and subconscious.

This mixing board of programs is the conscious mind and subconscious, which, in their total volume, can be called the law of correspondence of the individual. The behavior and character of the individual result from this total volume. This is his aura, the world of his everyday life. This is what he draws from, what he works with and what he lives with. Beyond this, nothing is possible for him, unless he creates further programs that are then—once they have taken hold—again active through him.

Therefore, the human being can be compared with a computer that, however—as mentioned before, this is the difference to technical computers—compiles its own mixtures, in order to embellish many a thing externally, presenting it as if it were the ultimate.

If a person has turned away from God and His commandments, then he will use his mixing board in many different ways. He will also use it as the potential from which to control others, and will try to control his fellow people, that is, to implant in them a part of his own potential of correspondences, of his world of programs, and project it into them, so that they do what he, the projecting person, wants. The sinful programs are designed in such a way that they always strive for what is considered good and worth striving for in the world: "Divide, bind and rule." This can be done only with the sinful programs, since they do not respect the freedom of one's neighbor.

In order to find our way out of the whirlpool of our sinful inputs, out of the web of the ego we have spun ourselves into, we should ask for the help of the Christ of God who calls our attention to our active sinful aspects each day. They speak to us when we get upset, when situations, conversations, encounters and much more bring us into turmoil. By way of the path which Jesus, the Christ, showed us, we will find our way out of what divides, binds and rules, in order to reach the principles of the divine laws which, in one phrase, are: "Unite and be," which means, be a brother, a sister, to your neighbor, then you are consciously linked with God as well.

If we want to take the steps to our true origin, to divine love, freedom, wisdom and justice, then this means the following for us: Recognize yourself in your irritation, repent and clear up your sinfulness and no longer commit the negative you have recognized.

*If we are not willing to recognize
and clear up our correspondences,
we can be controlled*

We penetrate the world of our programs by way of our five senses, because it is mainly our five sensory organs that give the impulses for the programs stored in our conscious mind, subconscious and soul garments.

The most important sensory organ is the organ of sight. It is connected to the powers of Love, Mercy and Patience. These three basic powers of God are the filiation characteristics, the foundation upon which to take the lawful steps toward the commandment of love, "Unite and be." If we have sinned against these three basic powers of God, against the filiation attributes, then we also transfer our sinfulness to the four natures of God, which are the further basic powers in us: Order, Will, Wisdom and Earnestness.

In other words, because we have turned away from God's love, we create our own egotistical love, the self-love, that results in the lack of mercy and in impatience. With these three reversed forces we also affect the four natures of God, the other four basic powers in us, by making disorder out of Order, and by instead of fulfilling the divine Will, asserting our self-will as the standard and criterion for our life. And instead of letting ourselves be inspired by our divine heritage, which is the divine Intelligence, we create programs of the intellect. Instead of dealing with our life on Earth seriously and attentively, we become slovenly and intolerant. This is what follows the shadowing of our divine heritage, from the origin, the love, all the way to disorder.

Nothing happens by chance. Every look to here or there triggers sensations and thoughts in us. What does this look, this moment, as it were, tell us?

If we want to figure out aspects of the world of our sinful programs via our sense of sight, we could briefly rest our eyes on an object or a person, that is, on whatever caught our eye at that moment. If we pay no attention to the usual stream of thoughts, we will soon become aware that we are controlled by aspects of the world of our own programs. They bring us into communication with those energies that resemble the momentary control through our programs, because like attracts like and expresses itself, that is, reveals itself.

An example: We experience a fellow person who talks very skillfully and convincingly, who knows how to draw the attention of everyone present to himself with eloquence and wit. If envy stirs in us, then we have activated at that moment of annoyance a part of our programs of envy, which immediately enter into communication with our inputs of envy in the soul and in the stars.

Something similar occurs when we come into communication with the world of programs of another person, for example, with someone whom we, in a previous incarnation or in this one, infiltrated, that is, programmed, in a certain way. Our feelings and thoughts tell us what lies behind these momentarily active programs of envy. In this particular case, for example, it could be that we once manipulated and betrayed this particular person with our eloquence.

As mentioned before, we can feel and think only because certain programs communicate with the same or like energies, which we ourselves once created. We can speak and act only if the same or like programs are in communication with our sending potential, or with the sending potential of another person, whom we have infiltrated. It is only via communication that we set free the mechanism for countless communication reactions.

If we are not willing to recognize and clear up our sinfulness, that which is against God, we can be controlled, that is, influenced, by other forces that bear the same or like things in them, so that we are no longer ourselves, but other forces work through us. In this way, our character profile changes; the mixing board of our sinfulness grows and with it, our negative communication, our law of correspondence. With additional inputs, we then create a huge network of communication, through which we can be inspired and programmed.

Through our personal inputs—together with those that were further propagated via projections—the person's sinful sending and receiving potential extends over the whole Earth, all the way into the purification planes, where the discarnate souls live.

Base souls influence human beings via their programs of addiction

Based on the principle of "sending and receiving," also called telepathy, the following can take place in the network of cause and effect:

A person who failed to resolve certain learning tasks that life set before him—that is, who pushed aside or repressed things instead of clearing them up, who blamed his neighbor instead of recognizing himself—clings, also for lack of energy, to the "harmless," to the pleasures and attractions that life on Earth has to offer. Among other things, his life consists of partaking of culinary delights that become an addiction more and more. As soon as he sees unusual foods or even merely thinks about them, he craves them; all his thinking and striving is geared to this—he must have them, otherwise he cannot think of anything else.

The addiction to alcohol is an even more obvious means of repression and of numbing oneself. In the end, the alcoholic is no longer choosy about what he drinks. He cares only about the effect: a state of consciousness that disconnects him—all the way to unconsciousness—from the "normal" feelings he has in life that are unbearable to him.

Gluttony and drunkenness are extreme programs of desires and of life on Earth, behind which lie failure, inferiority complexes, blaming others, feeling misunderstood, disappointment about others and much more. Such programs of addiction can be a great potential of correspondences, that is, of sinfulness in the soul, which also imprints the person.

The action of excessive eating and drinking is the same as sending and receiving. Addicts can be influenced, via the principle of sending and receiving, by correspondence fields that are identical or similar to their own correspondences, their sinfulness. Fields of correspondences are fields, accumulations, of negative energies that indicate the character of a certain correspondence, of a certain human weakness or wrong attitude, a sinful reversal of polarity. Wherever there are fields of correspondences, the corresponding, the base, souls are not far away.

Addictive people can also be influenced by earth-bound souls to abandon themselves to culinary delights and to drink corresponding beverages. These are the souls that, via human beings, feed off such pleasures vibrationally, because they are similar in their sinfulness, their correspondences and addictions. Therefore, souls with the same correspondences can emit to such addicts, projecting their own passion and greed into them. They stimulate the world of their correspondences, the world of their projections, that is, they influence a person's thoughts and senses, for example, his sense of taste and smell, so that the person increasingly craves culinary pleasures and corresponding drinks. By way of smell and taste, via the sensory world of the one addicted to drink or food, such souls then satisfy their own food addictions and cravings.

The same holds true for excessive sexuality. Such influence is also exerted on the insatiable, excessive sexual world of those who are oriented toward sexual pleasure, often by souls that, as a human being, lived a life similar to that of the person they approach. Again, it is, "What the person sends is what he attracts": the same forces and the same souls with the same and like dissolute sexual passions.

Many a person is besieged or possessed by souls which, via the human addictions and other compulsions, draw energy from them and gratify their all-too-human needs. They let these souls take a part of their life energy.

We should realize that a tree stays lying as it falls. This means that the soul is the same after the death of its physical body, only of a different substance. In the beyond, it has the same desires and passions, the same cravings for a life of passion and the addiction to pleasures. However, these cannot be gratified in the soul realms, since it no longer has a physical body.

Many people abet the urges, the greed of the addicted earth-bound souls by following their passions, their excessive addiction to pleasure and sexual excesses without restraint, and without asking, "Who, actually, am I? Is this compatible with a good character?" Or, "What would Jesus, the Christ, say about this?"—because even people who indulge their passions often call themselves Christians.

This explanation, too, is a part of the law of correspondence and of projection. Sin emits and attracts the same and like forces. The soul that has been attracted by a person then projects its desires into him by injecting into his world of communication, into the network of his sin.

Living in a world of pictures—
Fulfillment of our desires through souls?
The great danger in "harmless"
picture games

There are ever more people who live in pictures. This means that in their thoughts they create an imaginary world that is shaped by their desires. For example, they create a fantasy picture in which they are a good-looking man or a good-looking woman who is courted by an ideal partner. With this ideal partner, who becomes more and more concrete, they then have an intimate mental exchange.

The partner in this picture responds more and more to the desires of the producer, who creates his world of pictures like a film. This goes so far that in this film the person who is living in a world of pictures visually dines with the dream partner, organizes with him, again visually, visits to the movies or the theater, and other pleasant things. Later, passion comes into play. The producer of the pictures visually lives the sexuality with the imagined partner, who is totally responsive to the desires of the producer.

The person's world of images becomes ever more intense and extensive. In many ways, it is like a film reel, on which all the pictures can be called up again, which transport the producer into a world where he leads an amusing life with his partner that corresponds totally to the world of his desires.

In this way, the person creates, through his thoughts, imaginary forms, including the form of his partner. It is a thought form that the producer created and set into motion with his feelings and thoughts, but also with his body posture. The more often the producer enters this imaginary world, the more real it becomes.

"Wonderful—a dream come true," some may say. But here, a warning is expressly in order. Because this all-too-human dream world conceals a danger—very specifically, in the form of a soul. And this can be only a base, earth-bound soul, because a soul with a higher degree of illumination would never lend itself to this.

Someone who sends out wishful thoughts, at the same time projecting them as pictures into the atmosphere, into the sea of countless pictures of thoughts, desires and cravings, can attract souls. A soul then slips into the thought form created by the producer, and through it, acts on his body, fulfilling for him what he craves.

The well-known statement in "The Sorcerer's Apprentice" by Goethe, "The spirits that I called I cannot now get rid of" contains truth. A soul or even several souls, which are like the correspondences of the producer of the thoughts, were attracted by him, that is, called up by him. The one who has called them will indeed not get rid of them so easily. The producer is then bound to all these souls, not only during this life, but as a soul in the beyond as well. This binding to the souls that were called remains and obligates him to fulfill a return service, if the soul of the imagined partner—or only one of several such souls— is in the earthly garment, that is, a human being.

People who live in pictures dissociate themselves more and more from their fellow people; they linger longer and longer in their own imaginary world that satisfies them, because the pictures they created correspond to their world of desires and to their ideal partner. In this way, such people lose their sense of reality and let their own life pass by unused.

Lately, even the darkness is making use of this imaginary life for its own malevolent purposes. Apparently, via such and similar violations of the law that are totally against the commandments of God and the Sermon on the Mount, the demons mean to get hold of the negative energy of people via their sensory world, in order to expand their possibilities of influencing people. It isn't enough that through movies, television programs, popular songs, productions of the sex industry and much more, we people are enticed into entering a dreamworld of pictures—lately, an imaginary life is offered even via computers. It is possible to produce these directly on the screen, and then participate "live," so to speak, in order to pleasurably indulge in letting everything be done that one wants, in terms of desires and passions, sex and other excesses. The one who avails himself of this possibility will not at first notice what he has gotten himself into, except for being drained of energy. But the bill will inevitably be presented to him when his soul leaves the physical body.

The person who looks a little into the spiritual background of these developments can only shudder. The particular "appeal" of such games lies in the fact that there are invisible "fellow players," who participate extensively and "heat things up." The one who lets himself be lured into this dead end may find it very difficult to break free from the inflamed fire of the senses. Only the one who realizes what goes on here, and is aware that in so doing, he becomes an energy supplier and servant of dark powers, can perhaps liberate himself from this spell and influence, with the help of Christ.

It is erroneous to believe that our thoughts as well as our desires are "duty free." The "duty," which we may have to pay if we are not alert and let our negative thoughts and desires have free rein, can be quite high. Based on the principle of "sending and receiving," any deviation from the law of selfless love can, through a chain of actions and reactions, end up in a dependency on souls or in the camp of the dark powers.

Via films, videos and audio tapes of all kinds, via the written word in many magazines and books, many people—including adolescents and children—are stimulated to enter into an imaginary world of sexuality, but likewise of violence, war and destruction, and to become active there in their thoughts. Whatever romps about on this wavelength, hungry for energy on the invisible level, is attracted by the excesses of human compulsions and passions. The producer of the pictures will not remain alone in his world for very long.

The way to God consists in recognizing the base humanness and transforming it by clearing it up with the power of Christ. This is why God gives us commandments but does not forbid. Wherever something is forbidden, nothing can be cleared up; instead, it is repressed. But what has been repressed continues to live on—perhaps in the world of fantasy or pictures with invisible fellow players, or rather, fellow culprits.

Thus, our thoughts, our desires, our passions and compulsions are far from being duty free. This is something everyone should consider who lets himself be stimulated, seduced, and drawn into a dead end through pictures in magazines, on television, at the computer, and in many other ways. The person who produces such material, who publishes it and makes it available to others, thus making many people and souls the objects of his own projections, will know after reading this book what he has caused and what he has inflicted upon his soul.

Another example:

Two people love each other; they cultivate an intense physical contact. One of them dies. After its disembodiment, the soul still has the same inclinations and desires as when it was a human being. In the one who stayed behind, pictures of their togetherness keep coming up again and again; often it is only the loving face of the deceased that comes up in the imagination.

The person keeps longing over and over again for the former relationship, also for the passion or the physical act. In this way, he can draw the soul of his former partner into his aura, so that the soul is very close to him. By emitting sexual desires, which are, after all, energy, radiation, the soul can make itself felt on the body of the person and build up and cultivate a physical contact with him. The person does not see the soul, but he feels it on his body.

Here, again, it is: Like can attract like through telepathy—based on the principle of "sending and receiving." The prerequisite for this is that there is an active correspondence present, through which souls can send, that is, they undertake their "injections," use the person and perhaps stimulate him to other things. This is then a projection.

We can escape such conditions only by becoming aware of who we are in the very depth of our soul: pure beings, noble, fine and good—images of God. Then we can decide what direction we want to give to our life on Earth. Do we want to continue to entangle ourselves in the web of our correspondences, of our sinfulness, or do we want to become free before the "harvest of our sins," our fate, breaks in over us?

Once we have made the basic decision to follow the path into the light with Christ, we can take the next step, for a start, by making a firm decision to no longer make such contacts, by watching our thoughts consistently and clearing them up immediately. This is done with the help and the strength of the Christ of God on the path of transformation, which He teaches us: Repent of your sins, ask for forgiveness, forgive and do not nurture these thoughts, these sins, any longer.

Without the help of the Christ of God there is no escape from these compulsions, from the law of sowing and reaping, the causal law. Only through the alignment with God and the fulfillment of the Ten Commandments and the Sermon on the Mount can we escape from this network of sins and from their influences.

Every expression of life is preceded
by a communication.
By analyzing our world of feelings,
we figure out what lies behind our emotions

Among the sensory organs, the sense of sight plays the essential role. Especially via the eyes, as already mentioned, many sensations and thoughts are awakened from the inputs that lie in the conscious mind and the subconscious, but also in the soul. If we do not put this mixing board of our programs in order, and if more and more energies influence our active programs, then they have a stronger effect on our nervous system. According to our own programming, we slide into a lower range of vibration, get irritated, become aggressive, perhaps even depressed, or illnesses appear. The restless soul and the disharmonious person are then shaken and jolted by fate.

Often, the first symptom of such a chain of effects and consequences is an unsteady, restless look. The eyelids begin to flicker; the eyeballs move rapidly back and forth. This shows that the whole person is restless and often lacks self-control.

Everything is communication. In all of infinity there is nothing static and nothing that is self-contained. As we have already heard, it is only through communication that we can bring our sensory organs into action, because communication is a flow of energy. All our movements are done via communication. Before we sense, think, speak and act, communications are already taking place. Whether we eat or drink—everything, absolutely everything, is communication. Before we touch something, communication already runs its course through the world of our senses, feelings and thoughts. Every eye contact is a communication contact.

If our glances always go to certain types of people, if we find them pleasant and worth imitating, then behind this is a memory from this life or a previous one. It is also possible that in a previous life we associated with such types of people whose nature is close to our own. Through our world of feelings, our inputs show us in manifold ways what lies behind such encounters.

If we want to explore the causes for our pleasant or unpleasant emotions, we have to analyze the world of our feelings. We question the pure or impure feeling, by letting the reactions of our feelings rise up into the world of our thoughts, in order to read from it what is at the basis of our emotions. The world of feelings is a fine plane of perception, which is more oriented to the soul and to the subconscious than to the world of our thoughts. We can explore our world of feelings and then analyze in the world of our thoughts what we were able to receive from the deeper layers of our existence. We then experience our correspondences or our positive memories depending on what the deeper layers signal to us.

If our sense of sight keeps drawing us to certain people, whom we find desirable, it may be that we set a karmic cord into motion that tells us what lies behind this in us. This karmic cord that we set into motion through our sense of sight is the communication cord through which the impulses flow and express themselves in feelings or thoughts. If we desire a person, then we immediately activate our senses of hearing and touch. We find out where the person lives, how he lives and under what circumstances. And so, we come into movement. We listen and seek.

The senses of smell and taste are the ones that control those people who like to eat and drink to excess. Here, too, the sense of sight dominates and determines the amount consumed.

Everything wants to tell us something, for everything informs via communication. It is not by chance on which particular object or on which part of an object our gaze falls on. Nor is it by chance that our eyes rest on a particular color or form for a longer period of time. It is not by chance that when our look falls on a person, it chooses a particular part of the body. We have to ask ourselves the question: What are our eyes drawn to? What does our sense of sight want to tell us? What is the cause?

We are guided together with every encounter, and this wants to tell us something.
By honestly observing the world of our feelings and thoughts, we can dissolve bindings with the help of the Christ of God

As long as we let our feelings and thoughts chase through our brain uncontrolled, we will, in time, be chased by these ourselves. We become unrestrained, passionate and compulsive. We go through our days without self-control, taking whatever comes our way. In so doing, we create countless causes each day, which sooner or later have their effects. Thus, we slip more and more deeply into the thicket of our sinful programs, into the confinement of our karmic straightjacket.

May the person who wants to change to the positive begin with himself. During the day, he should regularly take a brief pause in order to monitor the world of his feelings and thoughts in those situations that bring his emotions into turmoil. In this way, he responds to his fields of communication, the world of his programs, in order to find out what is behind them. It is only in this way that a person will come to know himself, and with this, his correspondences, which are his personal law, his aura.

Every day, our attention is called to our inner life through situations, through people, through different eye contacts, as well as through nature. Uncontrolled and unbalanced people often say, "I know myself." But who really knows himself? Only the one who for years—and at that, day after day—explores himself and, with the help of the Christ of God, undoes the snares, the sins, he himself created. The one who does not follow this path does not know himself, because he does not know about his own person-law, the programs of his correspondences; neither does he know how many people he has already influenced, that is, programmed, by planting his will in them.

Every encounter brought about by our communications network wants to tell us something. Yesterday, we met a friend; today, we meet him again. Between yesterday and today can lie worlds of programs, processes, which took place in the one, as well as in the other. Yesterday, we may have thought about our friend in a totally different way than today; and seeing him brings out totally different thoughts, totally different occurrences in us. Why? Because we are connected or bound to each other through aspects from our programs, of which these were active yesterday and today, those.

Every person is not only a cosmic being of light as seen from his spiritual origin; he is also a cosmic person, because through his negative inputs he is also connected to the cosmos—the cosmos of the Fall-realms.

Just like the cosmoses, every person is constantly in motion. The cosmic irradiation was different yesterday than today. According to its influence, other parts of our program world were activated yesterday than today. The majority of people simply pass over their encounters with such different worlds of feelings and thoughts, without ever asking themselves what yesterday and today wanted to tell them.

If we want to get to the bottom of the active programs that became noticeable yesterday and today, we should take a look at, and analyze, the various feelings and thoughts we had yesterday and today. In so doing, we must consider: The thought is merely the shell; the content is what lies behind the thought, what takes place behind the thoughts, namely, in our feelings and sensations. These are decisive, because unlike our thoughts, they are not easily influenced. The prerequisite for this is that we be honest with ourselves. If we want to get to the bottom of who we are, we must first analyze the world of our feelings. It discloses aspects of what was, until now, buried in the world of our feelings, where the causes for our unsated desires, passions, base inclinations or our inferiority complexes lie. What we recognize in ourselves, we should clear up with the inner strength, the inner light of Christ, and no longer do.

If the turmoil of our emotions is only slight and if our analysis yields only traces of envy and disparagement of our neighbor, then often an obliging word or a friendly greeting can dissolve what briefly upset us. A big help is that we link with Christ in prayer and ask Him for support and help, so that we can free ourselves from these burdening feelings.

Another situation, in turn, can reveal a much greater interplay between cause and effect. Two people meet. One does not like the other. He uses some harsh words, reproaching the other for an unresolved situation. The other one reacts in a similar manner. It comes to a sharp altercation. Both blame the other. What does this want to say to both? It is not the words that both have used when fighting each other that are important in analyzing their correspondences, but what lies behind the words, the feelings and thoughts; these indicate what is underlying in the individual, that is, what is active within the law of correspondence.

The purpose of being brought together may often be to offer both the possibility to clear up what binds them to each other. The one who examines himself, in order to recognize himself in his correspondences, will draw conclusions from the conversation and his behavior, to then follow the path of clearing it up. However, the one who continues to accuse his neighbor increases his correspondences in the law of sowing and reaping.

Therefore, if correspondences are stimulated, a magnetism is released: Like draws to like. The one meets the other so that both can clear up or expiate what binds them to each other. Even if in a particular case the share of guilt is greater in one than in the other—in the majority of cases both have reason to clear something up, because it is seldom that the blame is one-sided. Even the "innocent" victim thinks and feels, and his reaction, his thoughts and feelings, will hardly be only gentle and resigned to his fate.

Our karma comes to meet us in many different garments—through people, situations, problems, difficulties, or even through an illness. The karma—our own correspondence, an aspect of our soul debt—plants itself before us in order to tell us that it is now active. Our correspondence essentially says to us, "I've rubbed you the wrong way. Now, clear up your part." And through illness, an aspect of our karma, our personal egoity-law, expressly draws attention to itself and addresses us. The illness affects our world of feelings and thoughts and wants to have cleared up what it bears: parts of our soul burden, our causes which now came into effect.

Suffering, fate, illness, need and people whom we meet are all speaking to us, as it were; they are calling to us. Consciously or unconsciously, they are communicating with us through our correspondences so that we may analyze our part, clear it up and no longer do it. This is the path of self-recognition and clearing up our sinfulness, our correspondences, in order to attain a luminous soul and become a healthy, upright person of good character. The one who does not recognize his sins and does not clear them up with the strength of Christ will become his own judge through his inputs in the law of sowing and reaping.

Someone who looks for his own correspondence in everything that is unpleasant, in every irritation or anger, in suffering, need, illness and the like will find it. If he clears it up and no longer does it, he will no longer be subject to self-deception and delusion about others. In relation to the sense of sight, this means: Look and you will see yourself. In relation to the sense of hearing, it is: Listen and you will hear yourself. The sense of hearing, too, is in communication with all the other senses. None of the five sensory organs acts and works on its own. All the senses are connected with each other; each one is dependent on the others to a greater or lesser extent.

Via the nervous system, the five senses transmit their messages of sight, sound, smell, taste and touch to the body, which then reacts accordingly. The sense of sight dominates the four other sensory organs, for it is the sense that controls and directs and is a major factor when it comes to influencing the nervous system. If perception via the eyes is shut off because of blindness, the senses of hearing and touch take over this primary function. Every time a sensory organ is limited or eliminated in its function, another sensory organ becomes more active in order to compensate for the deficiency.

If a sensory organ is weakened or unfit, the person in question should ask himself what wrong-doing is behind this. The measure required to find his share of responsibility for his own physical deficiencies lies in his feeling, thinking and speaking, in his whole behavior. This is why Jesus of Nazareth taught us, above all, to figure out and remove the beam, that is, the correspondence, in our own eye, in our sinful heritage.

Character and lack of character,
positive and negative changes of
our character profile.
The individual's network of programs
becomes the world in which he lives

All the behavioral traits in our feeling, thinking, speaking and acting, in our passions and desires, can be summed up in the one word "character."

The person who has a good character is dependable; one can rely on him; he is true to his word—when he compares, it to the Ten Commandments and the Sermon on the Mount and it corresponds to them. The one that lacks character has lost his character; he is not dependable; one cannot trust him nor entrust anything to him. He is like the weather vane that turns as the wind blows. The one that lacks character goes along with the opinions and views of others. He has no measure of values. Therefore, he assumes what others say without checking it. And he takes the same line, in order to gain an advantage or to reach his goals.

From the first day of our birth onward, the five senses are gradually shaped. After a short period of time, perception via the senses already begins, as well as the development of life programs and behavioral programs. The tools of the senses gradually develop in the young person; they are his feeling, sensing, thinking, speaking and acting. These tools often carry out what is conveyed by our senses. Seen as a whole, this is how the character predispositions emerge that change during the course of our life on Earth—to a flawless character, to a mediocre character or to a lack of character, depending on the light and shadows that our soul brought into this world and how the person continues to behave. In this way, we create either more light-filled sides to our life—if we keep the laws of God step by step—or we create more causes because we keep moving about in the same thought patterns and speak and do the same things over and over again.

There is nothing static either in a positive or in a negative sense. Our five senses affect the world of our feelings, our thinking, speaking and acting; the world of our feelings and our thinking, speaking and acting, in turn, influence our senses. If this communications network is negative, that is, sinful, then we should break through it. We should use the energy of the day in order to undo, that is, transform, the bindings, the knots and threads of the network, with the help of the Christ of God. At the same time, we should establish communication with God and with our neighbor, which changes our character profile in a positive way. We acquire a good character and, consequently, also the corresponding physical shape.

If our negative programs are transformed into positive forces, then our body and our brain cells vibrate on a higher level, because we have programmed them with the commandments of God. Only in this way, will the positive power flow increasingly through our soul and into our person, reshaping us into a flawless character, into a person whom one can trust, whose word holds true.

The opposite happens in a negative sense. If the communications network is sinful, that is, negative—and we experience this when we monitor our thinking, speaking and acting—then we can expand this as well. This takes place if we continue to sin, by forming further sinful programs, more correspondences, or by reinforcing our communications network with what already corresponds to us, with our disparaging or aggrandizing behavior, which manifests itself in our thinking, speaking and acting. Thus, if we create more causes, if we expand the negative communications network, then our passions, our hatred, our envy, our animosity and the like will increase. These added aspects, that is, all the negative effects that we created from what was already present, affect, in turn, the world of our senses, which then reacts accordingly. This chain of causes and effects is then the course of our programs.

By way of his inputs, which are also contained in his soul, the computer "human being" is in contact with the stars that have absorbed the content of his programs. The network of all these events is what makes up the world of the individual's life—

his "spider web," his "plasma world." He is in communication with whatever he has programmed himself with, that is, what he has stored, and this is the state of his consciousness. Beyond this, no perception is possible for him, unless he changes his consciousness.

Via programs of curiosity:
stress, dissonances in the nervous system
and creating more correspondences.
There is an interaction behind
all occurrences:
Like vibrations come together and
trigger effects

The one who lives in his ego plasma will experience over and over again that his uncurbed senses are the driving force for many an imprudent word and many an inconsiderate act. Here are some examples from everyday life to serve in self-recognition and self-analysis:

Our curiosity programs can become a big plague for us when our sensory impulses, which are linked to our correspondences, sound in our ears, in our sense of hearing. Our nervous system, which is influenced by the world of our programs, comes into vibration via these correspondence impulses. The person begins to listen in on everything curiously, in order to find out what the other person is saying to his neighbor or colleague.

Curiosity can become such a strong motive force that the person in question feels compelled to register everything that is going on around him. For example, if a male colleague speaks to a female colleague, his warped sense of hearing impels the curious person to go and eavesdrop on what is being said. In order to find out the details of the conversation, he even intervenes in the conversation. If the conversation goes against his own ideas, he can very quickly become nervous. His sense of hearing then transmits this nervousness, the resonances, to his sense of touch. The person then starts talking, as it were, with the movements of his body. Stimulated by the external correspondence impulses, the correspondences in the soul garments of the curious person start vibrating more strongly. Whatever is stored in these soul garments that corresponds to the external impulses of correspondence is then expressed by the person concerned. This means that the curious person speaks himself.

Through the turmoil of his correspondences, which call up the dissonances in his nervous system and which are expressed in the most varying gestures and behavior patterns, the person gives off a lot of life energy. Based on his exaggerated way of viewing things, his extreme reactions and hysterical display, he gets into a state of stress and into dissonances, which stimulate further correspondences in him, so that as a result of his curiosity, he creates further causes.

The one who allows such things to happen, who continues to cultivate this condition, instead of analyzing his compulsion to hear everything, so as to find the root of this evil and then clear it up, accumulates negative energies, that is, sinfulness, which may break in over him at some point and trigger a blow of fate or an illness.

During our hectic times there are many diseases. One also hears about the most diverse pathogens that are affecting people to an ever greater extent. A pathogen becomes active in us only when we offer it the right kind of milieu. We ourselves are the ones who—through our feeling, thinking and acting, through our behavior—create the milieu in our body that corresponds to the pathogen, inviting it to settle in us.

For instance, the more we come into stress, the weaker our immune system will eventually become, so that the respective pathogen can feel well in our physical body. Stress always develops from wrong behavior. We are often undisciplined and not focused on what needs to be taken care of now. Our senses and thoughts are often here or there and not in the situation, not with what we are momentarily doing. Often we play down this condition by saying, "I'm just nervous." Or we say, "I simply can't concentrate." We seldom ask ourselves what thoughts and feelings, what correspondences, are hindering our concentration.

Through curiosity we become involved in conversations and situations, for example, that we then dwell on in our thoughts. This absentmindedness results in disruptions to our work, because we are not focused. The result can be mistakes or omissions, which get us into trouble or time pressure and can lead to more stress.

The one reading this book might now raise the following objection, "If that is so, then every wrong course of events would be because of me. It would always be solely my fault, even if others are also involved in the situation or matter." Let us remember what Jesus of Nazareth said, "Remove first the beam from your own eye ..." This means that we should first figure out what our part, our fault, our "beam," is, before we blame our neighbor, for example, our colleague at work. Our part is our beam, our neighbor's part is his beam, also called splinter.

Only once we recognize our part, our beam, work on it and remedy it, will we become aware of our neighbor's part, which must not always be as great as we initially thought. Then it would be the "splinter" in the eye of our neighbor. In any case, we should first look at ourselves before we blame the other for it all.

The law of correspondence says: Whatever irritates us, the same or like thing lies in us. All of infinity consists of sending and receiving, that is, of communication. If there is no correspondence in us, that is, no receiving potential for accusations, insults, suspicions and the like, such correspondence-agitators will not touch us. They will neither move nor upset us.

People who strive daily to make use of the energy of the day, to recognize the root of their sinful programs, to then clear these up with the strength of the Christ of God and no longer commit them, become even-tempered and balanced people, who attain a deeper perception, thus sensing where others need help. They will then help according to their possibilities. This is the selfless activity that comes from the root of the divine and not from a correspondence.

Once we become aware that in all of infinity nothing happens by chance, then the smallest and most inconspicuous thing that moves us has a meaning. For instance, if a plate or cup drops from our hand, this has a cause. Our senses and our thoughts that led to a moment of inattentiveness or nervousness are the causes—therefore, we, ourselves.

If, for instance, an object falls from the wall, this, too, has its cause. At that particular moment, vibrations were set free that triggered it. All occurrences are based on a interaction: Like vibrations collide and trigger corresponding effects. Such vibrations need not always come from outside; they can also flow from our correspondences, from the world of our senses and thoughts.

Another example: We are working in our house or apartment. Suddenly, we are distracted by a noise from the street. If this finds a corresponding resonance in us, then this correspondence will cause us to take a closer look. We interrupt our work to see what's going on. A stranger is having a fierce argument with a neighbor. What do we do? Some of the words in their altercation might move us to go outside and join in with a suitable comment.

Thus, via our sense of hearing we are led outside. With our active correspondence we now bring our part into the quarrel. Since nothing happens by chance, this behavior wants to tell us something. What did we hear from this controversy? Why did we go outside? Why did we intervene in the conversation? Our correspondences communicate with us via our thoughts. They tell us what lies behind our reaction. If the argument took an unpleasant turn for us, if we got upset and therefore continue to think about it—but even if we were "victorious" because our opinions prevailed—we can be sure that we have increased our correspondence potential through these additional thoughts.

Therefore, nothing happens by chance. Everything wants to tell us something. Every agitation comes from the correspondences in us. If we are irritated about words that flow from the commandments of God, then our irritation comes exclusively from our burdens, from the correspondences that were touched, and not from the words themselves, from that which unites, which is divine. Everything that upsets us is there to be dealt with and cleared up *in us*.

Another example: We meet a former acquaintance whom we haven't thought about for years. In him, as well as in us, correspondences are stirred up. Today, the stars have brought us together. Our behavior toward this acquaintance, our thinking and speaking, shows what lies in us. If we analyze our reactions, our thoughts and words, we will find the root of our correspondences. We can then clear up these with the help of the inner light, of the Christ of God, in order to become free of the guilt that still bound us to this acquaintance.

Desires, cravings, envy lead to alcoholism,
gluttony, sexual excesses, drug addiction,
even murder.
The causes: things not cleared up,
perhaps from previous existences.
Regression into past incarnations
is not lawful

The world of our programs has many layers and is many-sided. Just as no person is exactly identical to another, so are our inputs different. The one is envious, the other greedy, the next one is curious, and still another, addicted. The sensory organs stimulate the programming of the computer "human being" and the programs of the computer "human being," in turn, affect the sensory organs.

If the senses of sight and hearing are heavily burdened with addictive desires, cravings, with curiosity and envy, these egotistical components have an effect on the senses of smell and taste.

Based on the mutual influence of the senses of sight and hearing on those of smell and taste, and vice versa, the person concerned can hardly resist indulging in pleasures of any kind. These egotistical components can then lead to alcoholism, gluttony, sexual excesses, all the way to the consumption of narcotics. These strains on the senses also have a corresponding effect on the sense of touch, so that the person can become a sexual offender or even a murderer. The predispositions for such excesses can come from past lives, where the former person created causes that he has not yet cleared up.

We are on Earth to recognize our sinfulness, to clear it up and no longer do it. Our feelings and thoughts tell us what the causes are in us, but so do our five senses, which influence the world of our feelings and thoughts, thus showing us the negative aspects that lie in us today, at the present, that should be recognized and cleared up. We do not need to be led into past incarnations—a practice that is an offense against the commandment of trust in God, and is inadmissible according to the laws of the eternal Being.

What do we miss out on, if we do not find out what sin we committed in a former life against God, against ethics and morals, against our neighbor, that is, how deeply we have entered the mire of all-too-humanness? Are we curious? Do we perhaps want to delight in it even today?

If we are oriented toward leaving behind us the old and sinful, so as to strive for the new person who is free and fulfills the laws of God on a higher plane of consciousness, then we will not seek to take a look into the papyrus scroll of our past.

Here is an example for better understanding:

If a heavy and large chunk of rock hits us, we will be seriously injured physically or even crushed. But if only a small pebble hits us, we may feel a momentary pain, but we quickly get over it. It is similar with regression into past lives. If we perhaps become aware of the sum of our earlier offences, it is very hard for us to bear; we are constantly preoccupied with it in our thoughts and, because of this, we can no longer grasp the pebble that the energy of the day brings us.

A commandment of God is: Use the day, so that you may recognize the pebble from the massif of guilt from previous incarnations, clear it up and no longer do it. If we act according to the commandment, "use the day and use the moment," then the grace of the Almighty can remove a large portion of the massif from a former life, without our having to expiate it. For the one who lives his day with God, and thus, with the help of the law of correspondence, uses it to recognize a part of his sinfulness, clear it up and no longer commit it, walks toward God. God in Christ will then come several steps toward him, that is to say that through His grace and love for us, His children, He transforms the massif into light and power for the soul. This is the way to the Father's house, out of the wheel of reincarnation and of sin.

Whatever we register by way of our sensory perception and our thoughts with the help of the situations of the day can come from previous lives, but now, the strength is given us to repent of these sins we have recognized, these wrong attitudes, and to clear them up and no longer do them with the help of the Christ of God. We should not simply ascribe it to karma, by shrugging our shoulders in resignation and saying, "Whatever hits me is karma and therefore inalterable."

A Christian should know that karma, a soul guilt, can be recognized and cleared up in good time with the help of the Redeemer-deed of the Christ of God, even before the effect becomes active. Jesus, the Christ, showed us the path of purification, which says: Recognize your sinfulness, repent of it from the depths of your heart, ask your neighbor for forgiveness and forgive the one who has sinned against you. If you can still make amends for something—for instance, if there was physical or material harm done—then you should do this, insofar as this is still possible for you.

The prerequisite for this is that we no longer commit the sins we have recognized and instead, fulfill the commandments step by step. Our way home to the Father's house is the path of resolving the karma with Christ—and not resigning to fate.

"Subdue the Earth" does not mean:
Exploit it, torture the animals,
manipulate the plants.
The soul is attracted by its own
stored inputs

We hear or read over and over again that
we can sin against our neighbor. But we
also sin against the nature kingdoms.

Since we, the cosmic, that is, divine-universal,
beings, are in the earthly garment and our physical body consists of matter, of water and earth, as
human beings, we are also a part of the nature on
the Earth. Thus, our spiritual body is part of the
spiritual kingdom and the spiritual nature kingdoms; our physical body, however, belongs to the
Earth and to its elements of fire, water, earth and
air. Since we are a part of the Earth, we also bear
the responsibility for the Earth and for everything
that lives on it.

God spoke in the following way to humankind:
"Subdue the Earth." He did not say: Torture the

animals, ruthlessly exploit the plants and minerals; exploit the Earth to the point that nothing is left but a cadaver. Neither did He say: Poison the rivers, lakes and oceans and destroy the atmosphere that envelops the Earth.

What did the nature body person do with the commandment of God to "Subdue the Earth"? He did not keep this commandment. He became a defiler and thief of nature, a slaughterer of animals, whose flesh he tastefully prepares and pleasurably consumes. He has become a robber of raw materials and not least, a torturer of animals in the most diverse experimental laboratories where animals are tortured without mercy or conscience.

With these and further excesses of the sensual pleasures over thousands of years, which we committed and still commit today with our feelings, thoughts, words and deeds, we influenced and still influence our genetic make-up. Whoever believes in the cosmic law that like attracts like, knows that the genes are not excluded from this. Let us ask, how did the genetic material get into the genes? In the end, via transmission. At some point in time, the genes must have taken in the genetic make-up that we transmitted to them. According to the principle of "like attracts like," our genes are programmed with our character traits and features, which we then call our genetic make-up.

Whatever the genes carry, our soul carries as well. We pass on our sinful genetic make-up as well as our character traits to our children and they, in turn, to their children and so on. Over the course of reincarnations, the genetic material that we put into circulation attracts us again. Who or what is the motor for this? Is it perhaps our soul, whose stored inputs seek out, in turn, *its* sinfulness and *its* character traits? The principle is: Like inputs always seek out themselves. The inputs of our genes that we pass on to our children and grandchildren also lie in our soul. If our soul incarnates again in another time or era, then it will be attracted by its own genetic material via the communications network.

An example: A child is procreated that bears the genes of the father, of the mother and the inputs of the soul, which is still in the purification planes. If the genes of the former human being are active in the embryo, this soul can incarnate in its new body according to the principle of like draws to like. Thus, the soul seeks out the genetic material of its former physical body. This means that the spider again takes up the threads of its web, which, for it, is life.

Transplants, transfusions:
taking over foreign information

Life is consciousness, vibration, communication. Every person is, in his totality, the expression of his information, which is the same as communication. These then form the state of vibration, the consciousness of the individual. The degree of vibration, which is the same as the degree of consciousness, corresponds to the pictorial material of the soul, which shapes all the structures of the physical body, above all the genetic make-up, the genes in the nucleus of each of the many billions of cells of the body.

Science knows today that all cells are in communication with one another; they send and receive, especially the cells within one organ, in order to coordinate with each other and exchange information. There is also a constant flow of information to the control center of the brain.

To carry out this exchange, nerve impulses, hormones, transmitting substances and light

serve this function. In this way, the body immediately recognizes every foreign vibration.

So what happens in the case of a transplant,
but also of a blood transfusion?

An organ that is transplanted, or also a transfusion of foreign blood contains billions of foreign cells that obtained their information data
from the pictorial material of the donor's soul,
which are, in turn, their communication, that
is, the state of consciousness of the cell structure. They all radiate their specific information,
positive as well as negative. The negative information is nothing other than the burdens, the
karma, the negative programs in the body of the
person. Thus, a transplanted organ, as well as the
transfused blood with its particular body information—that corresponds to the donor and thus
differs energetically and in frequency from the
body and the soul vibration of the recipient—is
not compatible with them.

This inevitably leads to a chaos of communication or information in the body. The cells, which
until now vibrated on the same level and were in

tune with each other, all of which had access to the same basic information from the pictorial material of the soul, are now exposed to an unknown flood of information they can hardly cope with, since parts of the communications network of the other person were introduced into the communications network of the recipient. These, of course, do not fit in, since the worlds of the donor and of the recipient are each made up of totally different inputs, correspondences and programs. In particular, the personality vibration—called its "integrity"—which is active as a program in the brain, slips out of gear. A jumble of aspects from two different characters is the result, in which the one that is materially stronger—the one with the stronger ego—tries to assert itself.

With transplants and blood transfusions, the physical situation can be compared to a team of two horses, two energetic forces that are not coordinated with each other. One cell or cellular tissue sends out the message "stop," the other one "go," as it were, and the impulse cannot be answered. Tension results.

Therefore, it is not surprising when after a transfusion of foreign blood, a deep depression is often experienced, because the soul's pictorial material now has to take in foreign information that was transmitted to it and does not come from the programs of its own physical body. The recipient of this foreign information needs some weeks to overcome this shock. But since the lifespan of the blood corpuscles, the foreign substance, is a maximum of 100 days, its influence is limited in time and generally stops after this period of time. But hardly anyone asks what it is like for the soul of the recipient in this process.

In the case of a transplant, the situation is more dangerous, since the immune system is suppressed with medication so that it cannot perform its natural function, which is to reject foreign tissue, foreign information and communication.

Because of this, the foreign organ radiates and emits its very own programs or projections, as it were, for many months or even years, while the recipient is helplessly and powerlessly at their mercy. They overlay his programs and cause disturbances in them. Tension develops, which the soul of the host body tries to minimize and compensate for, by gradually taking over a part of the karmic information of the foreign organ and therefore, of the organ donor.

How much the soul suffers under this manipulation, this enslavement, cannot be expressed in words. It burdens itself with additional sinful programs, additional guilt, for which it is now responsible and the effects of which it has to bear. With this, the character of the person changes. The body cells, however, cannot immediately relate to this adjustment of the soul.

Once the foreign programs have been adopted, the organ donor, whether human being or soul, is tied to the soul and body of the recipient of the transplanted organ. This binding, which is based on the transfer of a soul guilt, will one day have to be dissolved by both. How this is done depends, on the one hand, on the content of the foreign information and, on the other hand, on how the host body, the person, continues to think, whether he actively uses this break in his life by foreign programs, that is, if he expands them—burdening himself more in the process—or whether the soul can keep these foreign programs latent, that is, in an inactive state.

Through this constant foreign influence, a continuous misunderstanding takes place between brain, body and soul. Again and again, organ recipients report about a feeling of strangeness in themselves that is also expressed in pictures.

If an organ is transplanted from someone who is merely "clinically" dead, who, in reality, is still in the process of dying, then it is possible that the soul of the organ donor stays close to the body of the organ recipient because the latter now carries a part of the information of its soul body. Through the communication of the foreign organ with the soul of the deceased person, it is possible that the recipient's body is influenced by the soul of the deceased.

Since the purpose of our life on Earth is above all to clear up our soul burdens, after a transplantation this task can sometimes no longer be fully realized, or not at all, because the vibrations of soul and body are no longer identical. The foreign programs mean an additional burdening that came about without any wrongdoing by the person concerned. The hopelessness for the soul of the recipient is accordingly great. This karmic link between donor and recipient will come to fruition in the soul realms or in a future life on Earth.

Hardly any of the participants, whether patient or doctor, will perceive any guilt given today's state of knowledge in medicine. The patient is often unknowing or incapable of decision; the doctors refer to the sanctions of their activity given to them by society and the churches, which consider the donation of an organ to be the highest form of love for one's neighbor. Whether it is done against better knowledge or out of ignorance—from the spiritual point of view, a karmic web is formed, in which the church leaders and all those who condone foreign transplants are bound to one another, whether they inform themselves about the physical and spiritual correlations or not.

This is why many a doctor is of the opinion that the natural feelings of many people who have reservations about, or even an aversion to, donating and receiving organs is justified when seen from within, from the viewpoint of the soul. They sense that prolonging life at any price, paid for with a bad quality of life for the rest of a person's lifetime and the possibility of even greater suffering in the future, cannot be the solution.

Gene manipulation—
A chess move of the demons.
By creating a homunculus,
a "Brave New World"?

G enes are the carriers of our genetic make-up; they are consciousness, life in concentrated form. Whoever influences genes interferes in life and thus, in the competence, the will, of God. The one who changes genes is responsible for immeasurably great suffering.

It is said that genetic engineering is one of the industries that secures the future of humankind. It is said that it will revolutionize the production of foodstuffs and medicine, placing it on a new basis that does justice to the changing requirements of the future.

Until now, it was Mother Earth who supplied us with everything we needed for the maintenance of our physical shell, our body. She gave and gives us nourishment as well as medicine for maintaining health and for healing us. What until now was done by the forces of nature should now be done by intervention in the genes. Giant corporations have their "rights to life" patented. Significant areas of our life are thus surrendered to the dominion of the makers of big industry and thus become dependent on them.

Until very recently, the accepted practice was that a person's genes, his germ-cells and the human embryo were protected against intervention and manipulation by science. The identity of the individual was to be preserved in this way.

However, it is becoming apparent that neither the holders of capital nor do certain scientists hold back, if something is "feasible," as long as it can be peddled to the people as "progress" and promises the corresponding profit.

So what promises are being made?
— The solution to the hunger problem: enough food for all.
— The solution to many environmental problems: so-called "bio-reactors" instead of dirty industries.

— The cure for many illnesses. It is said that almost all illnesses are "genetically conditioned" and that all we need are flawless genes to produce healing.
— The arbitrary prolongation of life: "genes of deterioration" and "death genes" are inactivated.
— The procreation and production of healthy children, as desired and made-to-order.

A person who looks at this listing critically will recognize that these are all promises for the fulfillment of desires that humankind has entertained at all times, because people have always wanted to escape the consequences of their own doing and not doing in an easy way. However, the law of sowing and reaping refers each person to the recognition of his own guilt and the necessity to clear it up.

Because of the complacency of the human ego and the ignorance concerning the laws of "sending and receiving," as well as of "sowing and reaping," the genetic industry was and is able to slowly but surely convince the population that the advantages of genetic engineering far outweigh the dangers.

What are the dangers?

In food production there are already genetically manipulated plants that are resistant to pests, microorganisms or chemical herbicides. In this way, the plants flourish despite a negative environment which can thus remain unchanged.

This raises the question of whether the new and artificial genes in these plants can trigger detrimental effects in people. Conventional medicine claims that from the very beginning of its existence humankind has been exposed to foreign genes and has become accustomed to dealing with them. Even in the intestinal tract, so they say, genes are digested, that is, broken down into their components.

Other medical doctors, however, report alarming experimental results, in which genes and gene fragments were found unchanged in the blood, even though they had already passed through the stomach and intestines. There are reports in medical circles that claim suspicious findings in which foreign genes seek their final storage place in the body, as if magnetically attracted. In the end, it is said that in this context, the behavior of "prions" is to be considered, which, for example, trigger the "mad cow" disease. They manage to settle in the brain and force their own programs onto the genes, although they are not genes themselves.

An evaluation of such processes always depends on the point of view of the observer. The one who thinks only along limited materialistic lines—according to the opinion of a doctor—consider proteins, such as the prions, merely as molecules that behave in a purely passive way. But if we think in spiritual terms, we are aware that everything lives, that everything has a vibration and a consciousness, including all the components of cells. Consequently, they can also behave actively and purposefully.

And among the scientists, there are already some who recognize many things and express their reservations when it is claimed that the end products made from genetically engineered plants are completely identical with normal, conventionally grown plants. The same goes for genetically engineered medications, whether they are produced in animals, plants or bacteria.

As far as it is known, direct manipulation of fetuses and human beings is limited to individual cases. However, when it does take place, the integrity of the personality as a whole is shattered. Soul and body can hardly communicate with one another anymore, because the soul, with the programs it has brought with it, has hardly any access to its manipulated body. The person concerned has hardly any possibility for evolution, for clearing up his negative aspects. His life has no further meaning; often, it is simply a state of vegetating away.

We have to then ask ourselves the following: If a body, a vehicle, so to speak, can no longer be directed by the soul, the driver, then doesn't the "empty driver's seat" invite others to sit at the wheel?

From a spiritual point of view, much could still be said concerning the consequences of genetic engineering, but that would go beyond the scope of this book. So let us simply raise some fundamental questions:

Why transplants, why genetic manipulation? Is nature, as the Creator made it, imperfect? Is the Creator imperfect and is the human being the alpha and omega of creation? Or are the proponents, the manufacturers and the executors incarnated demons, or so controlled by the demons that they no longer know that they, too, are children of God, that their inner being has also been created by the perfect Spirit who holds everything in His hands?

The human being not only wants to take the nature kingdoms into his "creation brain," but he also sees himself as the ingenious creator and master builder of a new world. Many a culture in past ages displayed a similar arrogance toward the great Creator-Spirit. This always led to their downfall.

The controlled ego that no longer sees its neighbor, but only wants to confirm itself, it does not consider that during the past thousands of years, humankind has exploited the nature kingdoms, tortured animals to the extreme and continues to do so. That nature is suddenly unable to give anymore what we have cruelly taken from her, namely a healthy life, is now being cruelly "repaid": She is being manipulated by the obsessed "creator," the human being.

The "great" petty minds, whose thought world consists only of "me, me, me," who feel neither respect nor a sense of honor toward the life from God, cannot know that everything is information and communication. Even when they mix their statements with many pompous and knowledgeable words, presenting this hodge-podge as the ultimate, it nevertheless remains an arrogant, unproven information.

The divine information that is in all things, God, the life, is to be silenced because the giant corporations want to offer life and sell it. The demons seek with all their might to keep the Earth as their home base and to create genetically engineered human beings as further energy suppliers. It is a matter of indifference to them whether those manipulated still find their way back to their original life or not. What is important to them is that each person strengthens his own ego and steps on those "below." This establishes the communication with the demons.

From the Demons' State, infiltrations and more information then comes on how to possibly create soulless people who merely serve as robots that are either controlled by the demons or in which the demons move in and out like rats in a refuse-filled sewer.

Whether, in time, becomes similar to a misshapen pig or fattened ox or runs around as a cow-person is of no relevance to the manipulators. What is important is that the home base of the demons is maintained. An implanted gene, no matter how it was engineered or prepared, bears information; it is a transmitter. Wherever it finds the same or like elements, nature or the human being will be manipulated accordingly, that is, programmed. The result of all this is certainly not a child of God, but a homunculus, like a robot, which no longer has any feelings or self-control, that is, no conscience, but is merely the instrument and transit station for the negative forces.

And that is supposed to be the beginning of a "Brave New World"? We will experience what God wants.

*A person with a heavily burdened soul
has no feelings for the suffering creatures.
What a human being does to the nature
kingdoms will fall back on him*

Many people simply live through their days. They hardly think about why they live, why they are human beings, why things go well today and bad tomorrow. They hardly think about why one person is healthy and the other born already sick. Many do not think—and often do not even know—that they have an immortal soul that bears within the highest ethical values, which the person should again develop, so that after the death of its body, the soul can return to the pure worlds, to the realms of the eternal Being, thus sparing itself further incarnations.

Because the majority of people have become crude and cruel, they hardly find access to what is around them: people, animals, plants and minerals. This brute human being, with his base characteristics, with his hard-heartedness, has hardly any feelings for his fellow people, let alone for the sorrow and pain of his second neighbors, his animal brothers and sisters, the animal world. People with heavily burdened souls can be quite ruthless when it come to promoting their ego, in order to reach a corresponding gain. They have no eyes and no ears for the suffering creatures, nor have they any feeling for the inner life of the plants and minerals.

On the other hand, a sensitive and luminous soul in a person, and the person himself, perceives the suffering of his neighbor, but also of the enslaved creatures, the animals. He sees the fearful look of the animals that are often fattened in confining spaces for the animal cannibal, the human being. The sensitive person who is turned to God hears the anguished cries of the animals, which are brutally cooped up in trucks and freight cars—often without water and food over long periods of time—and taken to the slaughterhouses, in order to gratify the senses of taste and smell of people who are concerned only with their body and their earthly well-being. The luminous soul of a person also feels how the Earth suffers when it is exploited and excavated, in order to offer the insatiable human being the life of luxury he demands.

The worldly person, who squanders the energies of his soul and body, needs ever more food. The gifts of nature are not enough for him. He needs the culinary pleasures that stimulate his senses to ever more excesses.

The person who leaves the divine cycle, by going against the commandments of God, needs ever more worldly bread. The Earth should feed ever more people and ever more people addicted to the pleasures of the palate. For this reason, the fields are overloaded with fertilizers and supplied with substances that ultimately, only harm people. Hardly anyone asks whether the Earth is still able to give. It must. The last drop is squeezed out of it.

An example: If a woman becomes pregnant year after year and gives birth to a child every year, what happens to her? She is deprived of too many vital substances, so that she may become sickly. And the children that are born from a sickly body are often more susceptible to illnesses or may even be born with an illness.

It is similar with Mother Earth. Year after year, she is expected to yield more food because the population of this Earth is growing and her affluent inhabitants turn more and more into gluttons and egoists, who claim more food and goods for themselves. The glutton becomes a culinary citizen whose sole concern is to give his meals the right seasoning. In this way, he burdens his senses of taste and smell more and more, which then crave even more culinary delights. This culinary gluttony also leads to excessive sexuality. In all this, the insatiable brute called human being, who craves ever more opulent foods and other excesses, forgets that he is overburdening his organism and promoting illness. If he then does become ill, he seldom says, "These are my causes."

At every moment every person shapes his character, and with his character, he shapes his body, through the inputs that come from his feelings, thoughts, words and deeds. It is not necessarily in this incarnation that we developed into gourmets and gluttons and lead a dissolute life. These characteristics can be part of the soul baggage we brought with us. But the term "karma" should not become an excuse for us to continue to indulge in our vices, passions and drives, because, with the help of Christ, we can recognize and clear up our soul burden in time.

With all these ego-addicted programs of our ego, we not only harm ourselves; the correspondence is constantly on the lookout to charm others into becoming accomplices. Behind this are the invisible negative energies that are called the "satan of the senses." It is the demonic, which lives off the sins of humankind and which establishes depots of negative forces, in order to tempt the unstable, weak and pleasure-seeking people to plunge into more excesses. The victims are then cleverly incited to transmit the microbe of their own vices into others—via projections.

These examples and indications show us what it means to build up correspondences, to work with them and to have an effect on our neighbor with them. If he is weak and accepts what we force on him, then we have programmed him. This is then the projection into the world of feelings of our neighbor, who works with it, thereupon creating more sins. He entangles himself more and more in the threads of our web and spins more of his own.

The entanglements are manifold, multi-layered and, in human terms, impenetrable. This intertwined and knotted tangle can be called the "thicket of the human ego" or "the jungle of the human ego."

The person who strives for the high spiritual ethics refines his senses and enters into communication with the law of God more and more

What a person does to his neighbor, including by projection, falls back on him. What a person does to the kingdoms of nature likewise falls back on him. Thus, whatever a person does to other life forms, he does to himself.

Jesus taught the following analogously: "What you do to the least of My brothers, you have done unto Me." The animal brothers and sisters are our second neighbors. They, too, sense and feel pain and suffering. For us, this means that whatever we do to the nature kingdoms, we are doing to the eternal laws of creation, to God, and that also falls back on us.

Everything that goes out from us, light or shadow, divine or sinful—both come back into us. Thus, we ourselves are light or shadow. Whatever we send out is what we receive and that is also what we are; it shapes our character, and our character, in turn, shapes our body. If a person strives for high spiritual ethics, for the actualization of the commandments of God and of the teachings of Jesus in the Sermon on the Mount, he refines his senses, thus, likewise ennobling the world of his feelings, sensations and thoughts, as well as his words and actions. His external appearance becomes upright and noble, his frame of mind, good. More and more, he enters into communication with the divine Being, the law of God.

The inner harmony, the peace of a person who has found the divine in himself, and has thus found himself, shows in his shell, the person, and in his surroundings.

True beauty comes from within; it is the luminous radiation of the spiritualized soul. A young and fresh body can be attractive. Whether in its later years it is balanced, noble and fine, whether the beauty can shine from within to without, is determined each day by the person himself.

Wise people who have overcome their correspondences with the help of Christ are mature people. They radiate self-confidence, calmness and spiritual beauty. This is also their behavior toward their fellow people. They are tolerant, of good will and open to everything that is good and beautiful. People with spiritual qualities also have fine features. Their gestures are refined and balanced. Their surroundings radiate harmony in color and form. The look of a person who is turned to God is open. His sense of hearing is turned within, to the divine Wisdom, from where he receives the impulses for his life.

The average person, on the other hand, is more oriented to himself, to his ego. Through his grandstanding, which the program world of his ego demands because it needs the supply of energy on a base, human level, the person becomes intolerant and inflexible. He becomes the advocate of his own personal opinion. He loves the intellectual ping-pong game of discussions and constantly wants to have the last word, in order to outdo his neighbor.

The ego-person, who lives in his egocentricity, is a person of the senses whose life is turned without, turned away from the commandments of

God, and who consequently sees matter as reality, as his life. On the other hand, the person who has turned to God sees that matter is transitory. He will not turn his back on it, but neither will he see it as the sole source of happiness in life.

The one who seeks will find.
Experience yourself in your
correspondences, and find yourself,
the Self, as son, as daughter, of the Eternal

The insatiable ego of a human being, which in all its expressions cries out, as it were, "me, me, me—always and only for me," creates our ego-world, the world of our programs, which can have such serious consequences for us. In the midst of our self-spun communications network, we sit like a spider lying in wait for its prey, and continue to spin ever more threads, but we never see beyond the limited horizons of our own network. We are—from the point of view of our consciousness—"merely a human being," caught in his programs, a prisoner in his own web, tied to all those whom he trapped and "wrapped up" with his threads of projection, greedy for "still more"—and yet, deep down, restless and discontent. The life in the web of programs is not the true life; it is not the freedom; it does not bring peace and fulfillment, for which every one ultimately longs, because the eternal spark of life is in the innermost part of our soul and the light of Christ, our Redeemer, has taken up dwelling in the very basis of our soul.

The spiritual being, the soul, is in every person. It is not of this world, but has come to the world in order to clear up as a human being in the brevity of years the transgressions it bears. Whether as a soul or as a person, each one of us will at some point in time—often through suffering and sorrow or a blow of fate—come to the limits of his thinking and be confronted with the question: What purpose does our earthly existence have for the life as a soul in the worlds beyond? One day, the hour will come when we start to think about death and about what lies beyond it. Many dismiss thoughts of death out of fear for the unfathomable. Others, advocate their opinion that death is the absolute end. And others ask themselves, "What if things really continue after death?" Or, the person begins to search, "Was this really my whole life?"

Anyone who has such and similar thoughts is advised to take his questions more often into meditation, into a deep and silent prayer in the inner chamber of his heart; for the answer to such basic questions concerning life which, in the end, no one can avoid, lies in ourselves. We will probably not receive the answer directly from the inner light of truth, but the following holds true, "Seek and you shall find." We may, for example, be led to books or to people who will answer our questions. We can receive a direct answer from the inner light, from the divine in us, only once we have mostly cleared away the rubble of sin that lies before the inner gate to the holy of holies.

The task of our life on Earth is to clear out what is turned away from God, our rubble, in order to again be able to live in the holy of holies, in God. Then we will not merely talk about God and present our personal opinion about God or about what we have heard or read about and that we assume to be right.

We need not only believe. Each one of us can attain his own God-experience if he is ready to walk the path which Jesus of Nazareth lived for us as an example, in order to grow closer to God:

Recognize your sins, what divides, and everything that is not divine. Experience yourself in your correspondences when, for instance, anger, rage or rebellion surge up in you. Recognize yourself when your nerves tense up and you become like a high-strung bow, so to speak, the bow of all-too-human wanting and urging, on which already lies the arrow of your correspondences that is aimed at your neighbor, in order to inject into him the poison of your sinfulness, to program it into him, as it were. For this poisoned arrow may lead to your being bound to your neighbor over incarnations.

The steps to overcoming the negative and that lead us to the divine in us are: Recognize your sinfulness, repent of it and clear it up, and do not commit the same sins again. Fulfill the commandments of God step by step, so that you may find your way to the life that is in you. Go through your days on Earth increasingly aware of the eternal power that dwells in you, increasingly aware that you are a citizen of the Kingdom of God.

By clearing up our sins with the help of Christ, we transform ourselves from sinner to "blessed one." Our senses become nobler and finer and our soul pure. We gain respect for our fellow people as well as for the nature kingdoms. We begin to treasure God, the life in us, and gradually become the treasure seekers who unearth the treasure of the divine, in us. Then we will experience that God is in us and that we are in God, because we are children of God, sons and daughters of the Eternal.

Recommended Reading

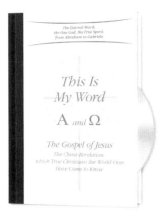

This Is My Word
A and Ω

The Gospel of Jesus

The Christ-Revelation,
which True Christians the World Over
Have Come to Know

Building on the "Gospel of Jesus," an existing extra-biblical gospel text, Christ Himself reveals through Gabriele, the prophetess and emissary of God in our time, the facts about His life and His teaching as Jesus of Nazareth—by explaining, correcting and deepening the words of the gospel.

From the contents: Childhood and Youth of Jesus • The Falsification of the Teachings of Jesus of Nazareth • Purpose and Reason of Life on Earth • Jesus Taught about the Law of Cause and Effect • Prerequisites for the Healing of the Body • Jesus Loved the Animals and Always Interceded on Their Behalf • About Death, Reincarnation and Life • The True Meaning of the Redeemer-Deed of Christ ... and much more.

Included with the book is an audio CD with the Eternal Word from the Kingdom of God: "The Call of the Christ of God" and "The Appearance," given in 2017 via Gabriele

1078 pp., HB • Order No. S 007en • Also available as an E-book

Words of Life
for the Health
of
Soul and Body

This book is based on the
Christ-revelation
Cause and Development of All Illness

This book is a revelation of Christ given through the prophetess of God, Gabriele. Thoughts and feelings have an effect on our body, parasites and other pathogens were and are created through the behavior of human beings themselves— all this and much more have meanwhile been confirmed by science. This book gives us detailed knowledge about the inner processes of people that lead to illness or health.

From the contents: The Separation from the Unity Consciousness and the Emergence of Matter • The Disturbances of the Magnetic Fields of the Earth and the Magnetic Streams • The Role of the Nervous System on Becoming Ill • The Law of Cause and Effect • Every Organ is Vibration, Color, Sound • The Chance Given in Reincarnation • The Quanta, the Spiritual Bearers of Energy ... and much more.

256 pp., HB • Order No. S 117en • Also available as an E-book

We will be glad to send you
Our current catalog of books, CDs and DVDs,
as well as the free excerpts on many different topics

Gabriele Publishing House – The Word
P.O. Box 2221, Deering, NH 03244, USA
Toll-Free Order No. 001-844-576-0937
www.Gabriele-Publishing-House.com